LOVE OF MONEY

ROOT OF ALL EVIL?

THE MOST DAMAGING LIE EVER SOLD?

DEVON S J MORGAN

*It is self-evident that there are
many evil acts that are not motivated by the love of money.*

In defence of money

*Money is a base subject. Like water, food, air, and housing,
it affects everything, yet for some reason, the world of academics
thinks it's a subject below their social standing.*
–Robert Kiyosaki

SOME OF OUR greatest success gurus, such as the late Jim Rohn, claimed that only about 5 per cent of people who retire in our wealthy Western democracies can do so and live in a state of financial independence. If this tiny and alarming percentage is factual, what part does a negative attitude towards money play? Why would so few achieve financial autonomy in rich democratic countries? What is powerful enough to stop so many people? Some of the answers are in this book. This book is not written with the presumption that it has all the answers.

This book was written to clarify some widespread, harmful misconceptions about money. It aims to present healthy alternative philosophies on this vital subject. The ultimate goal would be for some of the suggestions for changing our philosophies about money to become popular beliefs. This is important because opposing philosophies and emotions about money negatively impact the lives of millions, limiting their contributions to our collective prosperity.

Although the title of this book references the biblical scripture 1 Timothy 6:10, the entire content is not solely focused on blaming that scripture for widespread negativity towards money. Other strong emotional influences have contributed to the negative and often *conflicting* attitudes many people hold towards money. However, because religious beliefs are the most potent emotional force known to us—evidenced by the extreme actions they have inspired—they must be the most significant influence on those who adopt their negative dogma about money.

Is the love of money the root of all evil? No, the lack of money is the root of all evil. –paraphrasing Robert Kiyosaki, author of "Rich Dad Poor Dad."

The blame game is a universal occupation. Very few of us take full responsibility for our actions. We also tend to extend the philosophy of not taking responsibility for the actions of others. For example, we will use excuses such as "Someone led them down the wrong path", "It was circumstance that made them do it", and the ultimate excuse could be "It must have been the 'Devil' that made them do it".

The fundamental truth about how life functions is this: we possess the power of choice, unlike animals that must follow their programmes or instincts. With this power, we can accurately identify the source of blame or responsibility for our actions. The root cause of what we do is based on our level of intellectual, emotional or spiritual development. It is the failure to grow in these areas that leads us to often infringe on others' rights or commit evil acts. Recognising that we have the responsibility to develop intellectually, emotionally, and spiritually marks the height of human awareness and wisdom. The more we cultivate these two aspects of ourselves, the more effective we become as human beings; developing them is the foundation of health, happiness, and prosperity.

As we develop our intellectual and emotional capacities, we enhance the decisions we make, and better decisions, including our attitude towards money, lead to improved results.

I'm starting with the man in the mirror, I'm asking him to change his ways. And no message could have been any clearer: if you want to make the world a better place, take a look at yourself and then make a change. (Excerpt from the song, "Man in the Mirror" written by Siedah Garrett and Glen Ballard)

Our ultimate goal as human beings is to learn how to live a fulfilling life.

Money has become the most unfairly criticised tool we use for survival. It is often wrongly blamed for human behaviour. Money is simply an unrelated victim of misplaced blame. We have always had money, but it was not always in the form of paper, coins, or other inanimate items; yet when money consisted of livestock or crops traded during the barter system, no one claimed that the love of (food) cows or crops was the root of all evil. Incidentally, wouldn't it sound silly to say, "The love of food is the root of all evil"?

The *cultures* we develop establish the foundation for our thinking and also shape our *emotions*. It is these two human traits, thinking and emotions, that are responsible for our behaviour, not any inanimate objects like money, a knife, or a gun. Believing otherwise is like saying the tail wags the dog, not the other way around. The cultures we develop shape our philosophies, values, beliefs, superstitions, and rules. They are what shape our thinking and emotions, which lead to our actions.

Our *emotions* need to be educated just as much as our intellect! The attitude we *choose* to develop and embrace makes all the difference in the outcome of our lives! This cannot be emphasised enough.

Within Western cultures, a strong belief system rooted in religious values influences many people's thoughts, feelings, and actions. However, regardless of where our ideas and beliefs about money come from, we must recognise that it is the ideas and emotions we **choose** to accept that ultimately shape our behaviour. Human *thoughts* and *feelings* are the fundamental source of all evil.

Those of you who have taken the time to consider the different ways people respond to life's events may conclude that it is those who take full responsibility for their actions who are best equipped to remain unfazed by life. Suppose we elevate this perspective and accept responsibility not only for the events in our lives but also for the circumstances we find ourselves in. In that case, we arrive at the highest spiritual understanding of life. Recognising and accepting that we are ultimately accountable for our choices is the most empowering way to live.

Do you know anyone who never takes responsibility for what happens in their life? Think of someone whose attitude is like this:

no matter how many problems they face, it's always someone else's fault. Is this usually a very happy person?

It's not what happened that makes the significant difference in our lives; it's what we choose to do about it. – Jim Rohn

In the winter, the goose can only fly south, but human beings can go east, west, and north. We can reorder the entire processes of our lives, and we do this by the way we think! – Jim Rohn

---

This blame game has expanded to include money. People often believe that money has this extraordinary ability to 'get hold of us' and compel us to act. In truth, we should understand that money is simply a symbol of the commercial value and services we provide to others. Any action we take to earn money is driven by our thoughts and emotions from within. Our outer world reflects our inner world. Therefore, your relationship with money mirrors the person you have become inside. It follows that if what you do is care for people and you earn a lot of money from it, you likely provide significant, high-quality service because you cannot sustain a business without genuine service. If you failed to give good service, the market would eventually push you out, especially in a system of competition and free enterprise.

Why is this topic about money so important? Well, most of us will spend a lifetime investing our time and effort to offer some form of value in exchange for money, which we then use to pay for the things or values we desire. Money has become a vital part of how we live, survive, and enjoy our time on earth; therefore, we must develop an attitude towards it that benefits us and others. We should not have a negative attitude towards something that is an offshoot of our personal growth.

Money is something we primarily earn based on the value we contribute to the market or world of commerce. Most of us will not be *given* money to survive; we have to earn it. Harbouring deep negative feelings about money will hinder or restrict a person's prosperity flow. How many millions or billions of people around the world have had their abundance flow stifled, or worse still, never even begun, simply because they hold a negative philosophy about money?

The poorest populations in the world are often the most devoutly religious. Is there a link between poverty in devout Christian countries and the belief that *"For the love of money is the root of all evil"?* Is this far-fetched? What if we combined this belief with teachings against chasing after 'worldly things' and the philosophy of "this world is not my home, I'm just passing through"? What if we add, "It is easier for a camel to go through the eye of a needle than for a rich man to enter into the kingdom of God"? (Matthew 19:23-24, Mark 10:24-25, and Luke 18:24-25). Would such a mix of negative philosophies hinder a people's success flow? In Western cultures where Christianity prevails, there is a high level of underachievement or poverty among those who take everything in the Bible literally. The camel analogy illustrates an impossibility! How would this influence the success flow of those who accept it at face value?

Wealth can represent an extraordinary demonstration of our ability to serve others. What reward would such an effort not deserve?

Generally, countries with strong religious beliefs are usually not among the most technologically or commercially advanced. Technological progress is essential for significant commercial success because we live in a technological age. If you are still not convinced that there is a link between a country's religious devotion and its level of advancement, consider this: countries with theocratic governments rich in oil tend to be less developed than those with less oil but governments not based on religious laws. In some cases, they are less developed than countries not known for oil, such as Japan, for example. The reason for this is quite simple: how many hours would a religious population dedicate to creative thinking for technological and economic progress? Not as much as a less devout population. Less input usually leads to less output. Do some of these countries criticise the 'decadence of the West'? Does this suggest a negative attitude towards material wealth? Can you imagine what would happen if Japan or China had the oil resources these countries possess? Their discipline and *focus* would make them twice as powerful as they are now.

It is hard to deny that we usually attract more of what we focus on and invest our minds and energies in. The likelihood of gaining a lot from what we do not prioritise or invest time and energy in is very low. The pessimistic view we hold about money being responsible for many of our wrongdoings has become a scapegoat for humans' failure to develop themselves. It is a person's failure to develop their abilities to provide value, goods, and services to their communities or the world that can lead to them committing evil acts to survive. Once again, money is an 'innocent victim' of all the false accusations we make against it. We will only do wrong for it *if we fail to control our emotions* towards whatever we believe money can bring.

Once again, it is society's failure to instil a strong value system in some of its citizens that can lead a few to embrace the seemingly attractive option of crime and quick money. There is only one worthy goal for us as human beings: to learn how to live life well. *Part of living well involves creating value through goods and services for ourselves and others, which requires exchanging our time, talent, energy, and imagination for money.* This applies to most of us, unless you are Mother Teresa. If the philosophy of developing ourselves to bring harmless value to others' lives were a standard teaching across cultures, there would likely be fewer evil acts committed for money.

The story of Geoffrey Carrigan

Much of our ideas about money come from our beliefs; for instance, when I was at Sunday school I often heard the teacher say, "The love of money is the root of all evil." In other words, if you are a rich man, you are probably evil. And I sat there listening to that stuff for a while and really questioning my beliefs and my own soul. The other thing I hear people say is: "Well, if I become rich, then I will have more stress and I will have less time with my family." And yet when I look at my rich friends, people who don't have jobs but have massive amount of passive or portfolio income coming in, they spend much more time with their family, they have more free time, they live a better lifestyle, they are able to buy better healthcare and better education for their kids.
– Robert Kiyosaki, author of "Rich Dad Poor Dad".

Truth is a demonstrable reality, and the best way to demonstrate truth is by empirical evidence.

THE FOLLOWING STORY is so unbelievable that you'll have to take it on trust—despite not knowing me personally. However, if you can accept that truth is one of my core values (and I have witnesses who can verify what happened), then there's a valuable lesson to be learned from this event.

It all began during a conversation with a friend about the Bible verse: *"For the love of money is the root of all evil"* (1 Timothy 6:10). I was in one of my favourite moods—promoting logic and reason over belief. For clarity, when I refer to "belief," I mean the acceptance of an idea or story without proof. This story highlights just how fortunate we are that belief alone is not accepted as evidence in our courts of law.

I was having this 'discussion' with my friend Geoff about the Bible scripture concerning money... I said to him, 'If the Bible had said, "For the love of money is the root of some evil", then it would be accurate and we wouldn't be having this discussion.' He wasn't buying into this reasoning. He insisted that the Bible was correct.

You must understand that before this, I usually have brilliant conversations with Geoff about success and life. I have seen people become irrational and unreasonable as soon as the topic shifts to religion, but this is the worst case I have experienced.

I tried again... I asked, 'Can you think of any evil act that has nothing to do with the love of money?' He said, 'No.' By this point, the 'conversation' started to feel surreal; it seemed to me he had gone into a mental lockdown by switching off his reasoning capability.

Nevertheless, I persisted and tried once more. I asked, 'Is paedophilia or murder evil?' I used these specific examples because paedophilia has nothing to do with the love of money, and many murders have nothing to do with the love of money. What do you suppose his answer was? He said, 'No'.

I was stunned, and so were others. If I didn't understand simple human psychology, I would still be pulling out my hair trying to figure out why he said 'No'. So why do you think he said 'No'? The answer shows how dangerous it is to put any dogma or creed above the standard of reasoning. Our ability to reason is what makes us truly human.

He said 'No' because if he had said 'Yes', he would have to admit that the Bible was wrong! The irony here is that within the same Bible, there are scriptures that endorse wealth and contradict this one, yet only a few people know about them.

Why are scriptures that promote a positive attitude towards wealth so little known? All my life, I've only heard one negative scripture about money. If my friend and I learned about these other endorsements, what would our conversation be like? I can't say for sure because, as his response shows, people will go to great lengths to defend deeply held beliefs.

Now, look at some scriptures that speak positively about money, and ask yourself why these are not more widely known.

Proverbs 19:4
*Wealth maketh many friends; but the poor
is separated from his neighbour.*

Proverbs 10:15
*The rich man's wealth is his strong city: the
destruction of the poor is their poverty.*

Ecclesiastes 10:19
*A feast is made for laughter, and wine maketh
merry, but money answereth all things.*

What if these were the popular scriptures? Do you think it would change the entire ethos of the Christian religion?

The story of Geoffrey Carrigan demonstrates how powerful religion can be. It also illustrates the great responsibility that it has to make sure that its message serves those who accept its dictates.

We should all recognise the devastating impact that belief can have on people's lives. Suicide bombing is a prime example. This instance clearly shows how a person's beliefs can lead to visible consequences; however, the link between an individual's philosophy and their beliefs is rarely understood in relation to how it contributes to the destructive processes and outcomes in their life. This is true because many blame circumstances, luck, or chance for life's results.

Here is a principle repeated throughout this book: the scope, direction, and outcome of our lives are shaped by our *thinking*. The simple formula is this: what we know or believe influences how we feel, how we feel guides what we do, and what we do determines our results. So, what impact would a belief about money that is powerful enough to shut down our reasoning ability have on our financial future? For those who accept ideas about the law of attraction and metaphysics, do you think this would hinder a person's prosperity or wealth flow? Even if we use the simple formula above, it is enough to grasp the effect such an emotional belief could have on a person's life. It is acknowledged and accepted that our emotions drive most of our decisions. Countries in the 'developed world' with populations that largely embrace a religion teaching that the love of money causes evil tend to have very high levels of underachievement and poverty.

Considering the power of deeply held beliefs, there can be a link between such beliefs and poverty, which can influence a country's prosperity. What if a nation has a large proportion of its population that internalises this very negative and untrue belief about money? Would this cause them to avoid pursuing wealth creation? How many would be motivated to build financial empires, essential for growth in a capitalistic world? Long before I ever read the Bible, it was common for me to hear people say, *"Money is the root of all evil"*. Looking back, I now realise that this belief was widespread. I never once heard anyone say, *"For the love of* money is the root of all evil"*. In this edited version of the scripture, money and evil became twins. Some apologists for this scripture have often argued that using the word 'love' is essential to convey the true meaning. However, it is the use of the word *'all'* that makes the statement untrue.

Do not assume that the impact of this negative belief about money is limited to those committed to Christianity. Christian beliefs are part of the cultural fabric of our Western society, and culture, which is partly made up of the beliefs and values of a people, is absorbed like osmosis. I was aware of the 'love of money' dogma long before I ever read the Bible. It was a common, often repeated saying, and most of the people who said it were not practising Christians.

Whether or not many of us absorb negative biblical scripture about money, we are all exposed to negativity about rich people. Since there is a history of the wealthy and powerful oppressing the poor and 'powerless', it is easy for those who are not affluent to accept negative perceptions of the rich. Unfortunately, these perceptions have unintentionally been transferred to feelings about money itself. Many individuals with a negative attitude towards wealthy people have unknowingly created a false belief that ruthlessness and wealth are synonymous. They have not consciously recognised that money is inanimate and therefore blameless. It is essential to free money from the misconception that it is the root cause of people's evil behaviour. The true roots of such behaviour will be examined in the later chapters.

So, we now find that disliking the rich and powerful is the same as not wanting to be rich. This relates to having a self-image that suggests a person would feel uncomfortable belonging to a group they suspect of.

The ease with which politicians can gain political mileage by accusing their rivals of favouring the rich shows that the 'masses' have underlying negativity towards the rich and powerful. In effect, we have an 'us' and 'them' mentality within our culture.

It is generally accepted that we are more motivated to avoid pain than to seek pleasure. If the subconscious mind is conditioned to associate 'pain' with money, it will protect you by guiding you away from it. There are many related beliefs rooted in this false and commonly held negative view of money. It is pretty standard for people to say, "Money will not make you happy," or "Rich people are not happy." I have often had to explain to others that happiness and money are two separate matters. **As Jim Rohn taught, *"Money will only make you become more of what you already are. It accentuates who you already are. If you are inclined to drink a bit too much, with more money, you can become a drunk in style."*** If you were in the habit of hitting your partner once a week, with more money, you might do it twice a week. If you are a kind person with more money, you will become a philanthropist.

Money allows us to act out our most profound weaknesses or strengths, our most intense desires or fantasies. The point is, if you see someone you know behaving poorly after they come into money, they are likely acting on ideas and emotions they already held before receiving the money. You've probably heard someone say, "If I win the lottery, I would tell my boss where to stick his job!" Clearly, without money, they are harbouring these unkind thoughts. They are revealing their character and concealed thoughts.

**Financially independent people are
happier than those in their same income/age
cohort who are not financially secure**
– "The Millionaire Next Door" by Thomas Stanley
and William Danko.

Misleading 'evidence' against money

THE MISCONCEPTION THAT money causes much unhappiness and that wealthy people are not happy is part of the false evidence many gather over a lifetime. The truth is that poverty is the primary source of most unhappiness. Poverty can force people to be away from their children because they must work two jobs or long hours; therefore, they fail to spend enough quality time with their children. Poverty has led millions to emigrate and leave their children behind in search of prosperity in distant countries. There are stories where children from such situations have committed suicide due to depression caused by the absence of the love and care they are used to.

Poverty can deprive people of their dignity, pride, and self-worth. When they are poor and hungry, they may resort to desperate actions. Since I realised that many hold negative views and feelings about money, I have tried to gauge the extent of this issue. For many years, I often asked people, "Do you love money?" to see their reaction. The vast majority would say "No," and I would think, "How can you work for a lifetime for something you don't love?" Someone once told me, "If I get a lot of money, I will lose all my friends."

Who would want to lose all their friends? Such a negative belief about the consequences of having a lot of money can evoke intense negative feelings about wealth. If these feelings become ingrained in the subconscious mind, they could have a disastrous impact on the person's financial future. Years later, this same individual did something that sabotaged his economic prospects. He sold a rented property and bought a car. No matter what persuasion I used, I couldn't convince him not to sell the property. The option was available to re-mortgage the house, extract some money, and retain the property. Today, that property would have quadrupled in value, along with the rental income. Is this outcome linked to his negative beliefs about money? I believe so, and perhaps after reading this book, and using your memory and observation, you may reach the same conclusion.

Besides the question about loving money, I have also asked people for years if they would like to be rich. Most of them say, "No, I just want to be comfortable." Isn't there an implied suggestion in this answer that being rich would make them uncomfortable?

One of the most popular false evidence that people gather about the consequences of having lots of money is the idea that rich people are not happy. The interesting thing about this is that the people who are saying this are often those who don't know any rich people. So, how did they form an opinion about people they don't know or have never met?

They formed this opinion from watching television or reading newspapers, and the wealthy people they based their view on are mostly dysfunctional celebrities who are a small minority within this group. Unfortunately for them, this is a highly inaccurate representation of what a lot of money can achieve for people.

In the book *The Millionaire Next Door*, the authors highlighted research figures that state: "Two-thirds of the millionaires in

America are self-employed business people." This would mean that the Hollywood and sports representatives of the wealthy are in the minority since they don't qualify as self-employed business people.

So, it seems that there are three primary sources where people gather false evidence against money: the Bible, newspapers/magazines, and Hollywood. Because most people have no personal experience with rich people, their only sources of forming an opinion about the nature and characteristics of rich people are newspapers, magazines, and movies.

In many films, the wealthy character is often depicted as the villain, willing to do anything to achieve their aims. A typical example of this is the James Bond series. Many of us come to associate wealthy individuals with being ruthless through these kinds of films. However, in reality, ruthlessness can be found in all types of people.

All the ruthless people I know are poor!

THERE IS A common saying that states, "To be wealthy, you have to be ruthless." This is not true. Ruthless is defined as 'Lacking pity or compassion'. What does such a quality have to do with providing goods and services to the world? Some rich people give millions to charity, and some won't. Some ordinary people are kind, and some are mean. Being ruthless is not a prerequisite for becoming wealthy. The essential requirement is the ability to supply goods or services to enough people to generate substantial income.

Someone recently told me, "Having a lot of money can make you paranoid; you cannot be certain about people's motives. If you meet a woman, you cannot be sure if she likes you for your money or for who you are. This will force you to only associate with those who already have money." If you agree with this standard view, let me give you the good news: if you don't develop the skill to assess people's character accurately, you will face grief in your life, whether you have a lot of money or little. The high rate of divorce and short-term relationships proves the consequence of choosing the 'wrong' person. Once again, this shows that money is never the real issue. Our *personal development* always determines the success or failure of our relationships.

The false evidence we collect against money is only a small part of such evidence. We also gather so much false evidence about ourselves that it seems as if we don't know ourselves very well. Some of this false evidence resembles the idiomatic "elephant in the room". For example, it appears to be universally accepted that women are more emotional than men. So I ask: are men more aggressive than women? Yes. Is aggression based on emotion? Yes. From this, we might easily conclude that men are more emotional than women. However, in reality, women and men experience different intensities of certain emotions.

Additionally, in a macho male-dominated world, women are socialised to express softer emotions more freely than men. Men, on the other hand, express the aggressive aspects of their nature more openly. Therefore, ultimately, we are emotional creatures by nature, and at the very least, we are equally emotional.

The birth of money

COMMERCIAL ACTIVITIES BEGAN at the start of human civilisation. During the early stages of learning how to live in organised societies, we were much more self-sufficient than we are today. Individuals or families produced what they needed. Yet, the adage, "no man is an island", applied then just as it does now. Many would find themselves unable to produce everything they needed, so a system called barter developed. This was a straightforward system where a person would exchange goods with another. So, if someone had more goods or valuables than they needed or desired something different, they would trade with someone willing and possessing what they wanted. Even at a glance, this barter system had significant limitations for the progress of organised societies. Here are a few:

- Each exchange of goods depended on having goods of mutual interest.
- Since values (money) mainly were in goods and crops, they could spoil, and in the case of livestock, they could die, be stolen, be eaten by predators, or run away.
- Protecting crops and livestock was more difficult than safeguarding money.
- These mainly living, breathing representations of value and wealth used for trading were bulky and would hin-

der the ease of migration. Someone wishing to migrate would have to carry all their livestock (money) with them, often with significant and dangerous difficulty. Regarding crops (money/value), most of them would need to be left behind, and the migrant would have to replant them once at their new location. These logistical challenges ensured a disruption to a family's way of life; even planting vegetables required time to grow.

- Becoming a wealthy person was once limited to those who owned a large amount of land. This is no longer the case today.
- Being a person of modest means was also limited to only a few who owned a fair amount of land.

A historical point: restricted land ownership in Europe motivated the development of American civilisation.

It is clear that during the barter system, commercial activities moved at a snail's pace compared to today. For civilisations to develop, a faster and more convenient method of exchanging goods and services needed to emerge. Therefore, the creation of money was an inevitable and essential tool to enable convenience and promote the expansion of trade. Money also allows people to engage in a wider variety of trades and lifestyles. It simplifies the payment process, meaning individuals can work without worrying about being paid in goods or kind. They also no longer need to worry about transporting their payment. This is the basic story of money's origin; once it appeared, it was inevitable that its use would expand, and the ways of earning it would become more diverse and complex. Why? Because we are complex beings. The development of more varied and sophisticated earning methods *partly* explains the significant income and wealth gap among people.

One diverse way of earning money is through sport. Money drives the growth of sports entertainment as a livelihood or even a path to wealth. It's hard to envision the expansion of such industries without financial backing. Could you imagine football players queuing up to receive their wages in livestock and produce? How would fans pay for entry?

FIRST AND FOREMOST, money is an inanimate object. It has no life and therefore cannot influence anyone. It's the value we assign to it that determines its importance. In other words, it's the thoughts and emotions we cultivate toward money that are the real issue. We can foster feelings that view money as a beautiful tool to enhance the quality of our lives, our loved ones' lives, or the lives of others we care about. However, like flipping a switch, we can just as easily develop feelings toward money that are twisted and unhealthy. I've known people whose emotional relationship with money was so distorted and cruel that they denied themselves even necessities, such as clean food. One person I knew ate rotten food, and another cooked a chicken that had died from illness. He "wasted" nothing.

A good analogy illustrating the inanimate nature of money is that of a gun or a knife. These objects cannot commit evil on their own; they can only be used for malicious acts. They are entirely neutral. A gun or knife in the hands of a psychopath becomes dangerous and alarming, while in the hands of a farmer or a housewife, respectively, they are simply tools with practical uses. The same is true for money—its impact depends entirely on the intentions and mindset of the person using it.

- For most people, money signifies food, clothing, shelter, entertainment, and lifestyle. The majority have never committed and will never commit murder, rape, or other evils for money. Since I know that lying is not generally regarded as evil, and because it is the most common wrongful act people would do for money. A minority commits evil acts motivated by money. On the other hand, money has become a vital part of our interactions with each other. Because of its significance, it has generated strong emotions. So, what exactly is this thing called money, and why has it become so important? Here are a few pointers about money.

- Money is a medium of exchange; it acts as a facilitator, enabling us to trade our labour, talent, skill, knowledge, and imagination for convenient payment. This form of currency provides us with endless options for how we choose to use it.

- It is a measure of value – a practical way to pay someone the agreed amount for their effort. In a barter system, if the agreed value of labour was, say, fifty pounds (£50), but the employer had cattle worth more than one hundred pounds (£100), then you can see how impractical this would be.

- Money is how we measure the value a person contributes to a job, the economy of a country, or the world. For example, we might ask: how much is a top golfer, accountant, or labourer worth in the marketplace? The late Jim Rohn captured this idea well when he said, "We get paid for bringing value to the marketplace. You could be a valuable sister, brother, or friend, but to the marketplace, you could be worth very little."

- Money acts as a practical way to store our goods or energy (labour/services). In contrast, in a barter system, efforts were mainly converted into physical goods. For most people lacking valuables like gold, this by-product of labour would have a limited lifespan. Physical goods could not be easily stored for use as an old-age pension during the barter era. Such use would have been limited to a minority who owned land and could employ others to manage their crops and livestock. Today, the convenience of money allows us to work for half our lives and save our *energy value,* which may include our skills, creativity, imagination, and labour. This energy value we contribute to the marketplace is measured and stored as money, which can then be saved or invested to support us during the other half of our lives.
- In a barter system, you would have to work all your life caring for your livestock or crops, or simply working. This limited the range of lifestyles that people could enjoy. Money provides us with many more options for choosing our lifestyle.

General formula for earning money:
Money = Quality + Quantity of goods/services.

"We get paid for bringing value to the marketplace" is the secret to success that most of us pursue with varying results. No matter how large the sum of money that creating value for the marketplace generates, it cannot be regarded as evil or bad. This point applies only to the 'value' that is legal. Many legal things are harmful and can be considered immoral, such as cigarettes, alcohol, junk food, and guns. However, for various reasons, many people demand and seek such harmful items, and if they are not available, they will produce them. Nonetheless, for most of us, the value we contribute to the market cannot be deemed evil. People offer their labour, talent, and imagination to the world of commerce or government, and in return, they are rewarded with money. This process *can* help reduce poverty, illness, unhappiness, and crime. However, our 'free will' as humans ensures that there can be no fixed or consistent outcome. One person may transform a pile of rocks into a mansion, while another may turn that mansion into squalor.

All of this ties into the undisputed arrangement on this earth between human beings and Nature or the Source of Life that many refer to as God. This arrangement is encapsulated in this allegory told by the late Jim Rohn:

> *There is the story of a man who took a rock pile and in two years turned it into a beautiful garden. People came from everywhere to see it. One day, a man came by, saw the garden and thought it was fabulous, but he wanted to make sure that the gardener didn't take all the credit. He had this deep feeling inside that a lot of people leave God out. So he toured the garden and had a chance to meet the gardener. When he met him, he shook his hand and said, 'Mr. Gardener, you and the good Lord together have created this beautiful garden.' The gardener understood his message and his point so he said, 'I think that's true, if it was not for the sunshine and the rain and the miracle of the seed and the soil and the seasons there would be no garden at all.' But he said, 'You should have seen this place a couple of years ago when God had it all by himself!'*

Since I was about 22 years old, a desire to become financially successful has been awakened in me. It wasn't until I was around 32 that

I understood there is a connection between the dominant thoughts we hold and the results we experience. In other words, I had no idea that life was governed by laws and principles that can be applied or practised to achieve a desired outcome. If someone had asked me to describe how people succeed in life, I would have probably mentioned education, luck, contacts, and circumstances. The idea that our thoughts and desires are the significant factors would never have occurred to me. Throughout my 15 years of schooling, this was never mentioned once. It was only when I read Napoleon Hill's "Think & Grow Rich" that I became aware of the power of the intangible 'substance' we call *thought* or thinking. Now, it has become a never-ending journey to understand and master *thought*, which is the only thing over which we have complete control.

Controlling how we think is the most challenging task for many of us, particularly because we are also equipped with emotions. Strong emotions can become our 'instinct', which can, therefore, steer our behaviour much like animals' instincts guide them. In other words, we tend to rely on our emotions to make decisions rather than our intellect. However, I have concluded that the intelligent force that animates all of existence, which I call the Source of Life, has endowed us with the capacity to think and experience a wide range of emotions. This is based on the assumption that we did not will ourselves into existence nor design the way we are. Theories as to why we can think and have diverse emotions are elaborated in my first book, "The Undisputed Autobiography of God", the first non-religious book about God.

If most people on this planet made the simple observation that the style, substance, and *outcome* of animals, birds, and insects' lives are determined by their instincts or programming (with very little ability to deviate), and in contrast, the style, substance, and *outcome* of human lives are driven by our capacity to think, it would mark the beginning of great wisdom. From this, we should recognise that life, in general, is governed by laws and principles. A beneficial realisation would be that our lives are not controlled by chance and circumstance. To expand on the idea that our thought processes influence our lives, I propose a formula I haven't found fault with: what we know or believe (accepting something without proof) shapes how we feel (emotion or attitude); how we feel influences what we do (activities), and what we do determines our results.

If you accept this simple formula, it becomes clear how vital what we choose to know or believe is. It is even more important once you realise that the emotions arising from our choice of knowledge or belief can become the most potent part of our being. In simple terms, we are emotional creatures. Most of our decisions are made based on feelings. Therefore, if we assign a high level of importance to any idea or belief, the emotions linked to this idea or belief can harden and become unshakeable, immune to logic and reason.

"For the love of money is the root of all evil" is a notion that is heightened to the utmost importance for billions of people by being seen as 'The word of God'. Since such an idea is linked to money and is believed to come from a highly revered source, money naturally gains a greater emotional significance. It goes without saying that if we associate earning money with our most negative concept, 'evil', then money could acquire a very sinister and unpleasant nature. Simple logic suggests that we would not invest a great deal or an extraordinary amount of effort into something we believe could threaten our goodness.

For those of you who understand the nature of what is called the subconscious mind, you would see the danger of feeding it such a negative emotion about a necessity of life. The subconscious mind will steer us away from whatever it has been programmed to see as harmful or undesirable. The fact that *most* of the most *devoted* Christians are not very financially successful relates to this deep-seated belief. If you connect this with the fact that there is a popular theme within Christianity stating that "This world is not my home, I'm just passing through," plus the standard warning not to seek 'worldly things.' If you add the negativity about "love of money," this mixture of beliefs must influence how much such people would pursue prosperity. Considering how devoted religious individuals can be, if money or productivity were seen as worth some degree of devotion, prosperity would be a typical result.

How can people gain much from a world they are not very fond of and have only a superficial interest in? We will only gain much from what we genuinely care about. If people's focus is not on this world, they cannot get much from it. What chances are there that people with a strongly negative view of the world will enjoy above-average benefits from it? The answer would be, not very good. Any person or people who embrace the "For the love of money" dogma as truth will hinder their chances of prosperity.

From my years of reading, general observation, and conversations with people, I have concluded that opposing philosophies about money are pretty widespread, and the extent to which they are internalised will influence a person's financial future. People develop a negative attitude towards money from sources such as the Bible, movies, magazines, family, friends, and society in general. Here is another opinion that corroborates this:

"Perhaps the greatest shock I ever received was one I encountered when I began lecturing on success. I soon realized that many who attended my lectures were still trying to resolve the inner conflict of whether they should actually desire prosperity. Of course, they wanted prosperity – it's human nature. But they secretly questioned whether they should seek it, especially from a spiritual point of view. Surprisingly, many businessmen and women seemed to feel guilty about the whole idea of prosperity, though they were working quite hard to become prosperous, day in and day out, in their respective professions. But the question remained in their minds: Is poverty a spiritual virtue or a common vice? This discord in their thinking was creating a tug-of-war in their affairs, which neutralized their efforts to succeed, no matter how much work they put forth." – "Think and Grow Rich: A Black Choice" by Denis Kimbro and Napoleon Hill

---

Would someone or a group of people who lack a keen interest in this life consider engaging in an enterprise that could generate billions, employ millions, and provide valuable goods and services to the world? Would their negative attitude towards money cause them to focus more on the money itself than on the employment opportunities, goods, services, and improvements in human life that such an enterprise could bring? A mindset rooted in the love of money, often associated with the concept of greed, leads many to believe in 'too much money', implying that we should only seek what is 'reasonable' for our needs. For them, greed means wanting more than you need. This view, however, has several flaws. What if you decided that a million pounds is enough to satisfy your 'needs' and that this is a 'reasonable' amount? This idea overlooks inflation and fixates on the wrong aspect. In twenty years, this sum might no longer suffice because inflation will diminish its purchasing power. The correct focus should be on maximising *productivity* and offering as much *service* as possible to contribute to human effort.

The tendency to emphasise the wrong value extends beyond just money. On an essential subject such as food, we concentrate on how it tastes rather than its nutritional value. This is another widespread habit: focusing on the superficial rather than the real issue.

For those who believe that pursuing millions or billions is greedy, it is helpful to understand the difference between greed and ambition. I credit my late mentor Jim Rohn for this insight, who said, **"Ambition is when we pursue great wealth at the *service* of others, and greed is when we pursue wealth at the *expense* of others. Service to many can lead to great wealth and satisfaction."** It was the late Earl Nightingale who suggested that we are here to serve each other. This is obvious because without serving each other, there can be no great human civilisation. Who would want to go back to a time when we mainly did everything for ourselves, such as making our clothes and producing our food?

Why is money such an emotional thing?

*Let's begin with a simple reason why money is
so emotional: without it, you could go hungry!
This is particularly true if you live in a city.*

TO RESHAPE ANY negative notions we hold about money, we should hear this principle often: we are compensated for providing value to the market, and the quality of that value shapes how we feel about ourselves. You might think it's our feelings about the money we earn that matter most, but actually, ***it's how we perceive our abilities*** and the earnings they generate that influence our emotions. At the higher end, we often feel pride in our skills and the money they earn us; at the lower end, we might feel shame about ourselves or our abilities, or the absence of them, and the income they bring. All of this is influenced by a person's self-image, which determines what they are comfortable with.

Money is such an emotional subject because it is a direct extension of the person we have become. It reflects what we stand for in our commercial world. It shows how others perceive our value in business, and consequently, how they view us. This mindset gives rise to the desire to gain status, respect, and attractiveness, both commercially and personally. This is akin to Native American cultures of the past, where a man who owned the most horses was considered the most attractive to the women of the village. Such a man would have the pick of the women. The main difference in the emotions money evokes is that it allows for greater possibilities of achieving status, respect, and perceived attractiveness. We all have varying degrees of desire to be appreciated. It has been suggested that this desire to be appreciated is the most profound need we all possess. Perhaps you agree.

Globalisation is a facet of today's world that amplifies the opportunities for enjoyment through money. Beyond its economic meaning, globalisation can also be seen as the cross-border exchange of ideas, languages, and popular culture. It encourages the appreciation of different sights, landscapes, cultures, and lifestyles in distant lands. Television is a key instrument that stirs our imagination and emotions, influencing many of us to seek ways to experience those moments. The aeroplane facilitates travel to these exotic destinations, and money makes it all possible. Does this evoke a strong emotion within you for the beauty of money?

A compelling illustration that shows how money reflects the kind of person we have become is captured in the difference between being a millionaire and having a million. This idea is supported by statistics indicating that most lottery winners go broke within five years. A millionaire possesses skills and discipline used to build wealth. The late Jim Rohn shared his story of becoming a millionaire in six years, then going broke, and later realising that money was only ten per cent of his assets. His greatest asset was the person he had become, so he rebuilt his financial standing. If a lottery winner loses their million(s), it cannot be regained.

A person once asked me, "Why are people secretive about how much they earn?" He told me that he asked someone how much his job paid because he wanted to apply, but the person refused to tell him. I explained that money is an emotional subject and there could be many layers and a variety of emotions that influence people's attitudes. He then admitted that he doesn't tell his partner how much he earns because he is ashamed of his income. Here, within a minute of asking the question, he demonstrated how our *inability to increase our earning power* can have an adverse emotional effect on us. It is not the money he was ashamed of; he was ashamed of his inability to earn more money that would be suitable for his needs and desires.

People will tell you where they live, where they were born, how many kids they have, where they went to school, and where they work, but will not disclose how much they earn.

So, what are the other reasons that make money such an emotional subject? Why does it evoke such strong feelings in people? The first point that clarifies these questions is something obvious: we do not become emotional about anything we consider unimportant. It is therefore clear that billions of people have intense and diverse emotions about money because it is now an essential tool for survival. It is essential because it symbolises food, clothing, and shelter. This is obvious because physical cash has no intrinsic utility value. We cannot eat it, drink it, drive it, or live in it. So, people are not 'in love' with money; they are 'in love' with food, clothing, shelter, and a lifestyle.

Another reason why money has become such an emotional tool is the rise of individualism. In cultures with a strong village mentality, the desire for wealth among the majority of people in these societies would not be as intense as it is today. High levels of teamwork and sharing characterised the village mentality. It was a common belief in these cultures that each person was responsible for others. It was usual for houses to be built collectively. The late Jim Rohn promoted this philosophy when he stated, "Each of us needs all of us and all of us need each of us." This philosophy is not widely embraced today.

Individualism promotes the idea of being self-made. It increases the need for financial independence because, as already stated, there is no longer a village or team culture. Individualism has also fostered in many of us the desire for power and fame. Experiencing fame in the modern celebrity sense is a new emotion that our current culture has led many of us to pursue. This is achieved through television, movies, the internet, magazines, and books.

Access to lotteries and credit systems now allows us to develop feelings towards the possibility of living a lifestyle similar to that of the rich and famous. Many of us do enjoy such a lifestyle, but this also creates another emotion called 'envy among the neighbours'. The desire to live in what we consider a glamorous way of life can either excite or depress us. We feel excited if we think it is achievable, but it can be depressing if we believe it is impossible, yet it is the only way to live. Once again, it is clear that it is our per*ception* of what money can bring that matters, not the money itself. This mindset is a choice because not all of us assign the same value to how money is used.

Our current culture promotes the rise of the celebrity lifestyle and status. The intense interest many people have in the lives of celebrities has created a unique emotional link between money and fame. Many celebrities have been granted an almost divine status.

Numerous celebrities can endorse a product, and millions will buy it. This power that wealthy celebrities hold has elevated money and fame to a surreal level.

One of the most common emotions associated with money is the desire for financial security. Money can provide a level of safety that many of us dream of, but only a few will attain. The lack of worry about affording necessities or the stress of paying bills can evoke such strong feelings that they may compel us to act either remarkably well or exceptionally poorly, along with a range of actions in between.

A close relative of this feeling of financial worry is the fear of failure or poverty. This emotion tends to be stronger in cities than in rural areas. In rural communities, most people typically have access to land, making it easier to grow food, fish, or seek help from neighbours. In cities, there is usually a greater need for money to cover food and living costs, as these tend to be higher than in rural regions.

The strong demand for money in cities due to higher living costs, reduced assistance from neighbours, and the ease with which someone can become destitute all contribute to the fact that crime is most prevalent in urban areas. It is this elevated crime rate that fosters the association of *"The love of money"* with evil deeds. However, if a city experiences a high crime rate, it inherently indicates a *culture* that fosters such behaviour.

Cities are often the most impersonal places in terms of human relationships, and a lack of good human connections significantly contributes to crimes against individuals. Therefore, cities with the poorest relationships tend to have the highest crime rates. The intense emotions generated by fears of failure or destitution lead people to commit harmful actions in their attempts to obtain money. There are too many complex layers of emotion involved in this situation to attribute it to *"For the love of money."*

Another intense aspect of city living is modern-day consumerism. Consumerism evokes an emotion we call "keeping up with the Joneses." This is a desire to stay fashionable, to be accepted, or to look better and have more comforts than our neighbours. A characteristic of consumerism is that it aims to programme people to want more than what they need. We see this in things such as mobile phones, where people are manipulated almost every year to want the latest model. There is now a new model of car released twice a year.

Once again, *"For the love of money"* cannot be blamed for the consequences that can result from these phenomena, even if someone commits an evil act to acquire these things. Why is this true? Because before the current intense promotion of the message that we need these things, people didn't realise they 'needed' them. Consumerism instils new 'needs' in people, so the blame for the root cause of any evil act to obtain these new 'needs' must be placed at the door of the *culture* that conditions people to develop these new emotions towards consumer items. Buying one of each colour of a single product, owning several dozen designer trainers (sneakers), and having various models of automobiles is a relatively recent phenomenon. This attitude is one of the manifestations of consumerism.

Once we moved beyond defining wealth solely by livestock, crops, and gold, wealth assumed new, unprecedented dimensions. As a result, many individuals now possess fortunes worth tens of billions of pounds. This level of wealth often provokes confusion and resentment among many people. Commonly, terms like "ridiculous amount of money" or "stinking rich" are used as negative expressions to describe wealth. The more ways we create to earn money, the more people will see these methods as not being 'work' or not deserving of the pay they receive. There is also resentment towards the high wages of sportspeople, company executives, and others whose value is often misunderstood by the general public.

To many people, the question of how one individual can be worth billions or millions of pounds remains a mystery. This 'mystery' has also stirred envy or resentment – how can someone be paid so much or hold such a high value?

Ode to beautiful money

PART ONE

THIS DOES NOT suggest that our monetary system is perfect or cannot be improved. No system we create will be flawless. This ode is not about the system itself, such as tax laws or money not being backed by the Gold Standard. It is solely about the *tool* we call money.

In the areas where there is no substitute, money is king.

As established, money is merely a symbol of the values associated with things like food, clothing, shelter, and other items we consider interesting or enjoyable, such as paintings, music, and games. Therefore, paying homage to money is equivalent to paying tribute to all the essential and desirable things we need or wish to enjoy as human beings.

If we examine this in great depth, we find that human beings are the only creatures on this planet with a culture that requires us to work for others and to earn money, which functions as a medium of exchange. All other creatures are self-sufficient or are programmed to engage in communal hunting for food; for most animals, this constitutes the entirety of their activity.

No matter how far back you go, you will never find a human society where anyone, apart from young children, had a free ride. Everyone had to work to eat. This also applies to the animal kingdom. Each animal works and gets fed (paid). There are only a few exceptions to this rule. In some insect kingdoms, the queen doesn't work at all for food, and in our human kingdom, we also have a similar situation.

Our capacity for inventions and expanding the human experience ensures that we will need to spend money on more things. Our ability to broaden our experiences is one of the qualities that distinguishes us as human beings. Therefore, there is a direct connection between having enriched human experiences and the need to earn money. The more we enjoy the outcomes of expanded experiences, the less capable we are of being self-sufficient and the more we rely on money, as well as the genius and labour of others. For example, how many of us can make an aeroplane, car, mobile/cell phone, or television? To be truly self-sufficient and require little money, we would have to limit our human experiences. Life is more enjoyable when we broaden our experiences. Money has become an essential part of this wonderful equation.

Some religious groups and individuals restrict their participation in society by distancing themselves from many activities, yet they still require financial resources. And once again, money is wonderful because, at its core, it stands for food, clothing, and shelter.

We expand the human experience through activities such as stargazing, diverse fashion, numerous sports, games, skiing, skydiving, gliding, flying, snorkelling, deep-sea explorations, movies, documentaries, recorded music, surround sound, and many other human innovations. All these enhancements are born from human imagination, talent, and energy. This human effort comes with a cost, and money remains the most convenient and appealing tool to make it all possible. It is unlikely that accepting livestock as payment for an extraordinary invention would provide the same level of motivation as the convenience and utility of money.

It would be difficult and impractical if we paid modern-day professional sportspeople in a barter system, without using money. Just imagine the nightmare scenario—seventy thousand (70,000) fans queuing up to attend a football match with chickens or goods to pay for entry! Can you envisage the logistical nightmare of collecting and storing such payments? What if some of the players were vegetarians? Just imagine how messy, unpleasant, and time-consuming it would be to pay everyone concerned. This nightmare scenario highlights how essential money is for facilitating the expanded human experience.

Modern life often confines many of us to long working hours, leaving little time for other activities that matter to us. Money can offer the freedom to live in a way that is often considered the ultimate form of life — the freedom of choice. It enables us to go where we want, see what we desire, develop new skills like learning an additional language, acquire what we wish, and choose where to live within a broad range of lifestyles. Money also makes it possible to spend quality time with our children and families, which is essential for building successful families, communities, and ultimately, nations.

The availability of money frees your mind to concentrate on achieving your goals. If you know that your expenses are covered and you are relieved of the worry that comes with meeting your debts, you can devote all your time and energy to achieving your objectives. – "Think and Grow Rich: A Black Choice" – Dennis Kimbro and Napoleon Hill

---

For those who understand that our relationships are one of the great enhancers of life, you would appreciate the value of broadening our associations and making friends with people. This is a wonderful aspect of living that money can facilitate.

Money signifies food, clothing, and shelter; in that sense, we have always relied on it. For centuries, farmers cherished the soil and livestock; they took pride in their productivity and the resulting fruits of their labour. Now that our labour's outputs have been converted into money, we face a philosophical contradiction: we're told we shouldn't love the product of our labour—money. Yet most people openly declare they love a house, a piece of clothing, or a good meal, but they hesitate to say they love money. Such inconsistent thinking must stem from something deeply emotional.

This emotional conflict probably stems from religious teachings—specifically, the false and misleading words found in an ancient text called the Holy Bible, which governments and institutions have historically supported. According to Kersey Graves in his book *The Bible of Bibles*, "There are not less than eleven hundred and fifty pious effusions... claiming to have originated from the fountain of divine revelation." If we truly understood the significance of this fact, we might not hold such unquestioning faith in the words of the currently dominant Bible.

It is ironic and contradictory that the governments which endorse this book, teaching us not to love money, are the same governments encouraging us to be as productive as possible. Yet, we shouldn't love the product of what we spend most of our waking hours and a lifetime working for. Today's governments inherited religious institutions, just as we all have. In the West, where we don't have theocratic governments, it means we have people in charge who 'endorse' a country's religious tradition without understanding how Bible teachings influence people's behaviour. This assumption is particularly concerning with the teaching, *"For the love of money is the root of all evil."* (1 Timothy 6:10). Because we rightly have a separation of government and church, the responsibility is on us all to protect ourselves against such counterproductive and false dogma.

There must be a negative consequence to having a psychological conflict between working hard for something we believe is not deserving of love. The things we love, we will tend to care for, so perhaps those who are reckless with their money or make minimal effort to earn it have a psychological issue with it.

Unfortunately, we've moved away from the simple idea that work or added value equals wealth. We now disparage the outcome of our labour by accepting that we shouldn't love it. This belief offers no advantage to our efforts to be productive. "It is an ill wind that blows no good" is a fitting saying that captures this antagonistic contradiction.

---

*Money isn't everything, but it ranks right
up there with oxygen!* - Zig Ziglar.

Money can give us the option to avoid conforming to *all* of society's standards without facing 'punishment'. For example, people with wealth can set their fashion standards without the risk of being rejected from a job or social circle.

People with wealth are often given a platform to speak on issues that affect all of us, and what they say is taken seriously. From this platform, they can draw attention to atrocities and influence the attitudes of millions. They can galvanise people to donate money to prevent or reduce famine and to help repair the aftermath of natural disasters. What a beautiful thing money is.

PART TWO

The real love of money

Because of the vital role money plays in the game of life, we must develop an attitude towards it that benefits us. In this game of life and money, there is little room for errors in attitude; there are no time-outs, no substitutions, and the clock never stops. The significance of money lasts a lifetime.

Love can be our most uplifting, inspiring, and noble emotion. Why would anyone want to sully it by associating it with a base act such as evil? It is totally inappropriate to suggest that love is the root cause of evil.

You would be forgiven if you assumed that those who do evil things to amass money do so because they *love* it. **The things we love, we take care of and treat with respect.** Most of the people I am aware of who are involved in criminal activities for money do not treat it with care or respect, and live very narrow lives. Therefore, we need a new word or understanding to define the relationship that those who commit crimes have with money. Those who choose the criminal route to amass money are *often* those who lack the skills or mindset necessary to earn money legally. They mistakenly believe that because criminal earnings are usually faster than a job, it is therefore easier. They never consider the difficulty of living on the edge, avoiding detection, the stress from the fear of being caught, the danger of injury or death, or the cost of losing a part of their life through imprisonment. How much is a year or ten years of a person's life worth? This is a logical way to assess someone with an illegal relationship with money.

Ultimately, criminal behaviour is a learnt emotional habit that career criminals become comfortable with, and eventually, they become addicted to the risk and lifestyle. The proof of this is that many accumulate enough money to comfortably switch to legal activities that carry no risk of imprisonment, but they don't.

Remember, the cultures we create are ultimately responsible for our thoughts and actions. If, within the framework of our culture, we build a society that fails to educate some of its citizens with strong positive values towards their fellow men, then it is the culture that needs to be changed.

Humans are born with a mind that is almost like a powerful computer—capable, but lacking its essential operating software. If we fail to fill it with ideas and values that are beneficial to the individual and society, it will not remain empty. The mind's nature is to absorb from its environment. A helpful analogy is this: if you do not instil a strong value system in a child, they will still learn—just not necessarily from the right sources. Their beliefs and behaviours may be shaped by friends, enemies, television, films, and the internet. The bad news is that you—or society—may not benefit from what they absorb in your absence.

A prominent theme in much of Western entertainment culture is sex, deception, and criminal behaviour. The glamorisation of these themes in movies, music, books, and magazines can negatively influence impressionable minds by normalising such conduct. Over time, films and media can desensitise us to violence, dishonesty, and deviance. If you doubt this, consider how the glamorisation of smoking led millions to adopt a self-destructive habit. This awareness eventually led to cigarette advertising being banned in many parts of the world—a strong acknowledgement of the media's power to shape public behaviour.

The most common reason people turn to a criminal lifestyle is the influence of associating with those involved in crime or 'hero-worshipping' a criminal they have observed. Criminal acts committed to gain money do not necessarily reflect a *love* of money. Love is an emotion that goes beyond mere liking and involves a more profound *appreciation*. The question is: Does stealing or killing someone for money demonstrate a genuine extra appreciation for money? The answer is a clear no. Here are some philosophies that show a genuine appreciation of money and the proper spirit in which it should be earned.

- If you believe that money should be earned in a way that causes no harm to anyone and should solely serve others, you recognise the goodness and beauty of money.
- If you always give your best effort to earn your income to *add value to others' lives*, then you appreciate the goodness and beauty of money.
- Suppose you can recognise the incredible power of uniting human efforts of labour, skill, and imagination to reduce ignorance, poverty, suffering, and disease. In that case, you recognise the goodness and beauty of money.
- Suppose you can appreciate the role money plays in bringing images of life within the deep oceans, the beauty, and the majesty of our planet and the universe into our living rooms. In that case, you can appreciate the goodness and beauty of money.
- If you can appreciate the role money plays in producing books and documentaries to inform, then you acknowledge the goodness and beauty of money.
- If you credit money for enabling the worldwide sharing of music and films from various cultures, then you recognise the goodness and beauty of money.
- If you can offer credit in exchange for allowing us space to enjoy holidays with comfort, relaxation, and exploration, then you recognise the goodness and beauty of money.
- Money can offer hope where there was only despair. Some individuals may be critically ill and require life-sav-

ing surgery, medication, or care and attention that money can provide. I have seen many public appeals for help in this regard, and I wish I could assist *in a meaningful* way, but I have been unable to do so. I strongly desire to support those disfigured by sponsoring surgeries that could give them a chance at an everyday life. I also wish to provide meaningful aid to ease the despair that follows natural disasters.

- Money can bring light where there was darkness by providing electricity. Have you heard the story of *Thomas Edison*? He is the one credited with inventing the light bulb. How much do you think this costs? I don't know, you don't know, nobody knows. However, we are told that it took him ten thousand experiments before he achieved his goal. In today's money, it would have cost at least millions. What value has this brought to our lives?

- I am sure you have seen the effects of poverty that lead to starvation. Would you like to be able to donate millions that could help alleviate or prevent this from happening? There are times I've heard someone figuratively say that they were 'starving,' and I would jokingly suggest that they knew about starving because they had seen the word in a dictionary, seen it on television, or perhaps they had heard of it. Hunger is an unpleasant experience; it can cause dizziness and pain, yet it cannot be compared with an experience where every cell in the body is starving to the point of emaciation. Beautiful money can help alleviate or eradicate this experience from the human landscape.

- Money can uphold dignity for people in their old age. It's sad to see young people suffering, but it's even more heartbreaking when witnessing a destitute elderly person. The sight of a poor elderly individual starkly emphasises that those of us who wish to live long must prepare both physically and financially for the future. These goals are interconnected. Financial stability supports our physical health, and good health allows us to focus on our economic well-being.

- Some wealthy individuals have established scholarships to assist those who would otherwise lack access to higher education. Once again, money influences societal progress. Facilitating this within a barter system would be, at the very least, highly complex and challenging.
- Money can alleviate or eliminate homelessness.
- Did you know that the main reason marriages fail is often due to money problems? Here, we see how good money management and flow can act as a lubricant that keeps more couples together. What are the consequences of marriage breakdowns? They can cause children to become distressed and, in some cases, dysfunctional. This can weaken communities, societies, and ultimately a country. All of these issues can stem from *either* a lack of money or an unhealthy relationship with it. An important point related to this is that married people tend to be more successful than unmarried individuals. According to the authors of "The Millionaire Next Door," who conducted perhaps the most comprehensive survey of wealthy Americans' characteristics and composition, 95 per cent of millionaire households are married couples."
- We cannot care for our wives or husbands with just love and sex. There are five variables in relationships: social (you have to do things you share in common), spiritual, military (you have to protect what you have), political, and economic (i.e., no romance without financial stability).

- To reiterate, "In the areas where there is no substitute, money is king." Most, if not all of us, are obliged to pay for utilities. We cannot call up the utility companies and offer them thanks or love as payment. If you tried this, men in white coats might come and take you away to a padded room for the insane.
  - Money can instil pride in us; it can give us a sense of achievement because it is closely linked to the kind of person we have become.
- Money represents comforts.
- Money enables exploration and adventure. One of my aims is to purchase a large telescope so I can look into the universe. What about you?
- Money can resolve many sources of frustration and helplessness.
- Money empowers us and enhances our ability and influence to bring about change, to make a difference in our lifetime.
- Unfortunately, we live in a time marked by numerous injustices. Therefore, having legal representation is essential. Wealth enables access to top lawyers, providing additional peace of mind. It is common for someone to be wrongfully imprisoned simply because they cannot afford a proper legal defence.

Civilisations cannot achieve their full potential if most of their populations have a poor attitude towards money and productivity.

Healthy and unhealthy kinds of love

I love money! It gives me joy; I think it's funny, sexy, and powerful. But so many people think negatively about money. They live in fear, or dread, or embarrassment about the subject, and that for sure will limit their ability to earn it, and to keep it…My father is a good, honest working man, and yet, like 96 per cent of our population, he retired with insufficient funds. – Gill Fielding from the DVD, "Riches" (She appeared in Channel 4's *The Secret Millionaire*)

LET'S EXAMINE CAREFULLY what Gill Fielding has said. We should note two key points that have tremendous value: the first point is that there is a relationship between thinking negatively about money and the inability to earn and keep money; secondly, 96 per cent of people retire with insufficient funds. Surely you would conclude that there is a relationship between the two points? This gives added validation to much of what has been said so far.

You would be correct if you've concluded that you are being encouraged to love money without contradictions; that is, without a love-hate relationship with it. We all love money to varying degrees because we all love food, clothing, shelter, and a good lifestyle. Most of us don't realise this because we have been mis-educated to think of money as just a piece of paper, and we have also accumulated other negative associations with money that have already been mentioned.

If you're hesitant to describe your attitude towards money with the word *love*, consider that the amount of money you earn reflects your effort, and therefore, who *you* are. If you love yourself, then you should love the results of your effort. However, let's include a caveat at this point: not all outcomes of our effort are worthy of the word love because a person with a twisted or unhealthy mind may do twisted or harmful things. It is therefore debatable whether we should label certain feelings or actions as love. Suppose you have an eagle as a pet: you 'love' it so much that you cannot bear to be apart from it, and as a result, you refuse to let it fly. This is an unhealthy form of 'love' because eagles are meant to fly, and an eagle that cannot fly is unhappy. The question is this: Is this situation the eagle's fault? Of course not. You are meant to be the conscious, rational decision-maker in this relationship. We can also love others in an unhealthy way by being obsessive and jealous. This treatise advocates a healthy kind of love toward money that does not involve hoarding, refusing to spend on life-enhancing values, or eating rotten food to save money, as mentioned earlier in the context of true love of money.

A culture with an unhealthy attitude towards money, where cheap junk food is preferred over healthy options, is planting the seeds of decline.

Sex, money and immoral behaviour: Is our sex drive the root of *some* evil?

It was intentional not to use the expression *"the love of sex"* because it could be misleading. Sex and love are two powerful concepts that drive human life. They are the pinnacle of the human experience that regenerates life. On the other hand, *some* evil acts related to sex, such as paedophilia, have nothing to do with the *love* of sex or just sex in the strictest sense of the word.

So, the answer to whether our sex drive is the root of *some* evil is clearly yes. Sex-related crimes are widespread and well-known. Rape, which is probably the most common, is one such evil act. This act, often linked to a desire to dominate and humiliate another person, has nothing to do with a love of money or even a love of sex. Nor do they include heinous acts like paedophilia, serial killings, and many crimes of passion. Those of us with regular, rational common sense would not need to be convinced of this fact.

Those who understand life and human behaviour recognise that our sex drive is a crucial part of our decision-making. Taking it further, we see that sex is a primary instinct in all living beings. From this, it's clear why sex is used extensively to promote almost anything — because it works. It is also driven by our Western culture's preoccupation with sex. Evidence of this can be seen in how, in both Western and many Eastern societies, nearly all aspects of female anatomy have been sexualised — socialised into representing sex. In ancient cultures, a woman's breast was viewed as a gland for feeding infants. This truth persists in cultures where women often go bare-chested. In these cultures, the breast isn't seen as a sexual stimulant or as something to provoke molestation, as it might in the West or other regions.

There is a controversy surrounding what many Muslims consider a mistranslation of the Koran, specifically regarding the reward of

72 virgins in paradise for Martyrs – those, such as suicide bombers, who kill themselves (along with others perceived as enemies) in the cause of Allah. No scripture in the Koran was found that mentions the reward of 72 virgins. The nearest found was this:

Surah 4:74: *Let those (believers) who sell the life of this world for the Hereafter fight in the cause of Allah, and whoever fights in the cause of Allah, then is slain or gets victory, We shall bestow on him a great reward.* "

The truth about whether the Koran emphasises the reward of 72 virgins is not the main point. The key issue is that the idea of a reward involving sex has, in *part*, led some to commit evil acts because *they believe* it comes from scriptures they hold in high regard. This is a situation where sexual imagination can override moral judgement. How else could one explain any suicide bombing motivated by this apparent mistranslation of scripture? The exact role of the promise of 72 virgins in this context may be difficult to determine, but it probably influences the events. This serves as one of the strongest indicators of how powerful our sex drive is and what it can drive us to do.

So, what does our sex drive have to do with the pursuit of money? If satisfying a primary drive, such as sex, is a significant part of our decision-making process, why would the pursuit of money not be linked to helping us satisfy this primary drive? Do we have any evidence of this? There is certainly plenty of evidence to support it. Let's take the simple example of a boy wanting to date a girl and wanting to start a family. At some point, the boy will recognise the importance of money for long-term success in meeting his sexual and family needs. So, apart from satisfying his basic needs for food, clothing, and shelter, the need to fulfil his primary urge for sex and family would also be a fundamental motivation for acquiring the ability to earn money.

Now, if you accept that sex is a primary or basic drive that we pursue to satisfy, would this also apply to the criminal pursuit of money? Is one motivating factor for men involved in criminal behaviour also based on the need to fulfil their sex drive? It seems so. Why would it be any different from an ordinary law-abiding citizen? The difference is that one seeks fulfilment of this drive through having a job, while the other chooses an illegal route.

Furthermore, the depiction of the criminal lifestyle in films often carries a strong sexual undertone. This medium is influential. It frequently shows the criminal way of life as providing easy access to many attractive, alluring women as part of the reward. An impressionable mind might accept this, and if such a mind does not have a firm philosophy and attitude against crime, it is not a big leap for them to adopt such a lifestyle. This is especially true if they also see many people they know and respect living this way. Criminal behaviour is learnt, just like any other behaviour. Now, when we have a culture where criminal activity and sex are glamourised in movies as entertainment, such media can 'teach' or motivate an impressionable mind to become a criminal to attain this reward of sex and 'glamour'. Generally speaking, this influence will occur subconsciously.

All of the points above have strongly argued for a connection between men's illegal pursuit of wealth and the desire to satisfy basic sexual drives or fantasies. As previously mentioned, they choose unlawful methods to fulfil a primary drive that everyone shares. Films often depict powerful criminals surrounded by semi-naked women and constant champagne at their pool parties, and in reality, many criminals behave similarly. Men attempting to pick up women at nightclubs sometimes buy expensive bottles of champagne to entice them. However, in truth, most wealthy men do not act this way.

According to the authors of "The Millionaire Next Door", ninety-five per cent of millionaires in America are married couples. Do you think most career criminals are married? It seems like the opposite is true. So, what other lessons can we draw from this about the validity of the dogma, *"For the love of money is the root of all evil"*? You might conclude that if 95% of the wealthy are married, they were not driven to become rich by a desire to live a lifestyle many would consider immoral or decadent.

The perception from Hollywood that most millionaires lead self-indulgent, luxurious lifestyles is also challenged by "The Millionaire Next Door". The authors revealed: *"Most millionaire households did not have extravagant lifestyles."* This was supported by surveys showing that most millionaires spent far less on luxury items like cars, watches, suits, and other luxury goods or services than non-millionaires. All of this highlights the main message: Our lives are not defined by any inanimate objects, whether it's money, a gun, or a knife. We are the living, *thinking, emotional,* and breathing force behind our actions and reactions to life's events, and all of this has been shaped by how we were socialised from childhood to adulthood. If there is one message to take from all of this, it's this: It's a bad idea to speak ill of anything you desire, need, and find essential! We must eliminate our tendency to find scapegoats for our actions. This tendency to blame external factors indicates that many of us do not fully understand how life works, and we cannot fix what we do not fully understand.

Synopsis of our sex drive being the root cause of some 'immoral' behaviour

WHETHER WE LIKE it or not, morality is subjective. It's considered immoral to drink alcohol in the East but not in the West. It could be argued that portraying women as accessories is an immoral act that diminishes the human experience. However, the decision is yours. Here are some observations about behaviour that are mainly linked to the male sex drive.

- Most criminals or social deviants are men.
- Sex is depicted in movies as a type of 'reward' for criminal behaviour. This has influenced some men, at least subconsciously, to opt for criminal careers.
- Sex is our most powerful drive.
- Women are sexualised by our Western culture and are marketed as sexual 'accessories' in the promotion of high-performance cars and motorbikes. This manipulates our sex drive, a tactic also seen in films. Such mental programming encourages many men to pursue money legally to buy cars or motorbikes they cannot afford, to increase their 'sexual pull'. It also pushes men to pursue money illegally for the same purpose.

So, what lesson can we learn from the fact that people will commit both legal and illegal actions to achieve what they want? The realisation that people will do good and evil for money shows us that the common factor is *people*! Money is neutral. It has no life or energy that can compel us to act.

The pursuit of money and happiness

HAPPINESS IS RIGHTLY called the universal pursuit. Everyone desires to be happy. The likelihood of finding someone with a philosophy like, "I don't want to be happy," is, at best, very slim. Let us therefore consider the role money plays in the quest for lasting happiness. This is not about the brief moments of pleasure we all occasionally experience. Lasting happiness can be an elusive goal for many, but it is not impossible to attain. Happiness is a state of mind or a perspective on life that fosters feelings of pleasure and contentment. Enduring happiness does not mean experiencing constant pleasure and joy; life doesn't work that way. Instead, it involves adopting a philosophy and cultivating an attitude towards life that enables us to overcome life's setbacks and remain resilient.

Happiness, like most things in life, has various levels; just as pleasure varies in intensity. What if you aimed to live a life that offers life-enhancing levels of joy, contentment, and awe-inspiring feelings of happiness? Can money play a significant role in making this a sustainable lifestyle? Indeed, this does not mean it cannot be achieved without above-average amounts of money. Still, it suggests that maintaining this experience for a lifetime while stuck in a menial job is unlikely. Here is a quote I totally agree with:

A person cannot really be free if he is chained to a routine job most of his waking hours and receives a mere subsistence in return. If a person has to pay that much for existence, he is paying too high a price. — "Think and Grow Rich: A Black Choice" by Denis Kimbro and Napoleon Hill

---

Is the feeling of being free a key part of a higher and more intense experience of happiness? Yes! In modern societies, can we maintain this feeling without having the freedom to choose our lifestyle? Unlikely. How flexible can we be with our lifestyle choices without being financially independent? Not very.

Many may disagree with this because of a simple phenomenon: every level we exist on, both mentally and physically, can become normal and acceptable, allowing us to find some measure of happiness. This is related to the saying, "You cannot miss what you never had." Then someone might say, "You think that is nice, wait until you try experiencing this!" This could trigger a mental process where we begin to imagine higher possibilities and then engage in personal development to mentally and financially embrace the new vision.

An advanced experience of happiness involves living a lifestyle that provides intense, life-enhancing levels of pleasure, contentment, and awe-inspiring awareness of our existence. The phrase 'life-enhancing' is intentionally used to exclude anything harmful to the body, such as hard drugs, alcohol, smoking, and even some 'foods'. While many find pleasure in these and consider them essential to their happiness, this is an illusion because they often shorten lifespan and reduce quality of life. Ultimate happiness is an experience that endures throughout a lifetime, during which we optimise our physical and mental potential. This does not mean that happiness is a constant state of bliss; real life does not work that way. Nonetheless, it is impossible to fully realise our mental and physical potential when living in poverty or merely having enough to survive.

In modern societies, money is the tool we can use to create space and time for developing our minds and emotions through reading, listening to diverse educational audio recordings, attending educational seminars, and exploring this wondrous world. Our minds and emotions are the foundations upon which we can build a lifestyle of sustainable happiness.

Having to struggle to pay for the necessities of life is not compatible with living in a state of minimum stress. Having a lifestyle of minimum stress and fear is vital for achieving a lifetime of happiness.

Suppose our lives are structured like a treadmill, where just a month or two without work could jeopardise our home, our children's education, or our ability to afford food and other essentials. In that case, our happiness rests on a fragile foundation.

Money gives us the freedom to have many options to improve our quality of life and make us happy. If you enjoy relaxing on the beach, you can multiply this with money by visiting multiple exotic beaches around the world. If it is about spending more time with your family, you can do this with more style if you wish. If it is about attending ball games, you can attend all of them.

Money and happiness can be two separate topics. Why is this true? A person can have money and be happy or unhappy, and a person can have very little money and still be very happy or unhappy. The phrase 'very little money' is used because it's hard to imagine someone living in any modern society without money and still being happy. Here again, two experiences are shown that are at opposite ends when it comes to money; one is happiness, and the other is unhappiness. This also indicates that the common factor is always *people*, their attitudes and philosophies. It's never any inanimate object!

It makes little difference what is actually happening, it's how you, personally, take it that really counts. – Dr. Denis Waitley

THERE IS A common misconception that whenever celebrities have problems, it is related to them having 'too much money'. Those who believe this conveniently ignore the fact that most dysfunctional people they know are not successful, and many of them are poor. Recently, after the tragic death of the legendary and iconic singer Whitney Houston, a woman came into my place of business. After expressing sympathy for Whitney's death, her terse comment was, "Too much money." Money was not the root of Whitney's problems. If 'too much money' is a 'weapon' that destroys people, then thousands of individuals who have far more money than Whitney would be doomed to the same outcome. However, there is no evidence of this. Most wealthy people do not live out-of-control lives.

Money, guns, knives, or any other inanimate objects have no power to force us to do anything. It is also true, for the most part, that even the circumstances and events of our lives hold no *absolute* power over the choices we make. This is a truth that far too few of us understand or accept. This level of consciousness will take some time for the majority of us to develop. Until we reach this conscious awareness, we will continue to have a very top-heavy, pyramid-like structure of human achievement. This is why only a few will ever enjoy even a fraction of the pleasure that this spinning blue-white planet has to offer.

People who recognise and accept that they have at least some control over their circumstances are often the most successful. History is filled with stories of individuals whose lives show the truth about where the real power guiding our lives lies. Here are two such examples of people whose lives illustrate the reality of our control.

Oprah Winfrey

I don't think of myself as a poor, deprived, ghetto girl who made good. I think of myself as somebody who, from an early age, knew I was responsible for myself, and I had to make good. – Oprah Winfrey

---

Her life is well documented, particularly her childhood sexual abuse and her tragedy at age fourteen. It is pretty standard for women with similar experiences to be affected in ways that often limit their success in adulthood.

Oprah Winfrey's life shows that no outcome is fixed. She has transformed the hardships of her childhood into a remarkable success in her adulthood. She is now one of the wealthiest and most influential people in the world, who makes a significant difference in the lives of millions.

What is the secret to her success? It has something to do with her being a prodigious reader and a deep thinker. These activities and her life experiences shaped an attitude that was conducive to her having a natural affinity and empathy with the struggles of others. This became the cornerstone of the success of the *Oprah Winfrey Show. Once* again, we see a demonstration of the truth that it is our philosophy and emotions that are the deciding factors in the actions we take. We are in control!

W Mitchell

This is a man who experienced such terrible life events that they would have overwhelmed most people. In July 1971, he sustained sixty-five per cent burns when a laundry truck collided with the motorcycle he was riding. His face and hands were badly scarred when his gas tank exploded into flames. His fingers were so severely burned that he lost most of each of his ten fingers.

This major setback didn't stop or slow him down significantly. He remained active, and on 11 November 1975, he crashed a small aircraft he was piloting due to ice on the wings. This left him permanently paralysed from the waist down. Did this stop him? No. After two years, he was back in the game of life. He ran for Lieutenant Governor of Colorado and won. His campaign slogan was, "Vote for me; I won't be just another pretty face in the Governor's mansion." He turned a circumstance that would stop most people into an 'asset'.

So, here we have a man who had every reason to believe that life was working against him. He could have easily chosen to retire on his disability allowance and pension, and nobody would have criticised him. If he had opted for this, no one would have asked, "How come you gave up?"

What would you have done? Would you have dismissed this as just 'fate' and withdrawn from life? That is what most people would do. However, W Mitchell did everything I mentioned and much more. Despite his physical challenges, he started water rafting, got married, earned a master's degree in public administration, continued flying, became involved in environmental activism, and took part in public speaking.

W Mitchell is now a millionaire. He lives in California and owns a second home in Hawaii. So, what is the philosophy and attitude that have shaped him into who he is today? Does it align with the theme of this book, which states that our lives are shaped by the way we think and feel? Well, let's take a look.

His lectures are usually titled "Taking responsibility for change". The core of his message is often a paraphrase of the 2nd-century philosopher Epictetus, which was also frequently used by my late mentor Jim Rohn: *"It's not what happens to you, but how you react to it that matters"*. W Mitchell also said:

"Before I was paralyzed, there were ten thousand things I could do. Now there are nine thousand. I can either dwell on the one thousand I've lost or focus on the nine thousand I have left. I tell people I have had two big bumps in my life. If I have chosen not to use them as an excuse to quit, then maybe some of the experiences you are having, which are pulling you back, can be put into a new perspective. You can step back, take a wider view and have a chance to say, "Maybe that isn't such a big deal after all."

Philosophical musings on civilisations and money

Civilisation is the intelligent management of human emotions. – Jim Rohn

A civilisation is great to the extent that it can manage and educate the emotions and intelligence of its people so that we grow and become productive. However, its foundation must rest on an international morality of respect and appreciation for each of our rights.

THE STRENGTH OF any civilisation lies in its institutions and systems of learning that are established and developed. It can be measured by how well its cultures promote the health, success, and happiness of the people.

The fundamental foundation that would support people's welfare forever is having a productive population with a philosophy and attitude aligned with correct principles. What are these correct principles? They involve having knowledge and practices that align with the Laws and Principles of Nature. Why is this essential? It is crucial because the Laws and Principles of Nature govern us. We can begin with the fundamental Law of Nature that is vital for our survival, which is the Law of Nutrition. This law determines what we should or shouldn't eat.

The lack of awareness about this law is costing us significantly in terms of lost productivity. Most people die prematurely due to what they have ingested. It takes time and *money* to train each individual to become a contributor who can help sustain our societies. The premature loss of people can lead to brain drain, a decline in productivity, and a loss of intangible values such as relationships and emotional support.

We find ourselves on this incredible, almost never-ending journey called life. However, there is no clear indication that the leaders of this world share a unified philosophy about how we should spend most of our time. Our main quest should be to understand the full dynamics of Nature—learning how to live in harmony with it and reap its rewards.

So, what does all of this have to do with money? The foundation of our existence is based on how well we learn to utilise the raw materials of Nature, and this forms the basis of our commercial activities. Money is the tool we use to represent and measure our productivity and exchanges with one another. Productivity and commercial interaction are essential to the growth and strength of civilisation. Civilisations cannot reach their full potential if powerful institutions fail to teach financial management and wealth creation to the majority. Instead, many promote negative philosophies and attitudes about money—views that hinder the productivity and progress of large portions of the population.

When I began reading books and listening to tapes about the psychology of success, one common statistic mentioned was that only about five per cent of people achieve financial independence by the time they retire. This refers to a situation where a person retires and can sustain themselves financially from their resources. In this context, there is an implied suggestion that a retired person who is financially independent should be able to maintain a standard of living similar to when they were working, without relying on charity or goodwill. The opposite of financial independence in retirement is dependence on government support, inadequate pensions, the kindness of relatives, or assistance from friends or charitable organisations.

Over the years, I have pondered this five per cent rule and its implications, and my conclusion remains just as astonishing as ever. It suggests there is a ninety-five per cent chance of not reaching what can be considered a minimum requirement. This idea should be particularly relevant for those of us living in affluent democratic countries.

My instinct as an inquisitive person is to ponder the root cause of such a phenomenon as this five per cent rule. Is this phenomenon related to statistics that suggest that only about five per cent of people are serious readers? In addition to this, take a look at these statistics:

- *1/3 of high school graduates never read another book for the rest of their lives.*
- *42 per cent of college graduates never read another book after college.*
- *80 per cent of U.S. families did not buy or read a book last year.*

- *70 per cent of U.S. adults have not been in a bookstore in the previous five years.*
- *57 percent of new books are not read to completion.*

(Source: Jerold Jenkins, www.JenkinsGroupInc.com)

There is a correlation between reading and financial success, but exceptions to this rule exist. Oprah Winfrey exemplifies this point most publicly. Her diligent reading habit significantly contributes to her success. Once again, we return to the fundamental principle that influences our life's outcome: what we know or believe shapes how we feel; how we feel determines our actions, and our actions shape the results we achieve.

The scourge of poverty

*Poverty is like the weeds in our gardens. It does not need
to be planted. It grows as a result of our neglect.*

HAVE YOU EVER wondered why there are no common negative
sayings about poverty, yet so much has been said about money?
Does this make you think that perhaps we have been brainwashed
and miseducated into this way of thinking? Do you also speak ill of
money or wealthy people, yet never curse poverty? Considering the
devastating effect poverty can have on people's lives, don't you think
something is wrong with this picture? So, you know all the nega-
tives about having "too much money", but have you ever experienced absolute poverty? I mean, true poverty?

Did you hear the joke Chris Rock made about having to save
up to qualify as being poor? I cannot claim to know absolute or
rock-bottom poverty. We had enough to get by. I am one of seven
children, and we never starved or knew hunger, but there have been
occasions when we used salt to brush our teeth because we didn't
have toothpaste. However, I have seen absolute poverty where people daily rummage through the city's dump for food or anything

of value. Yet we have all seen absolute poverty on television, where people didn't even have rubbish to rummage through; they just starved to the point of emaciation and death. Have you ever seen this level of poverty or starvation in rich countries? Well, I have never seen anything remotely comparable to the effects of famine we have all at least seen on television. And this experience is always in poor countries.

Do you think many experiences could be worse than thousands of people dying from starvation and disease? How would you compare this with any difficulties you can imagine as a result of being wealthy or having "too much money"? These two realities are so far apart on the scale of human experience that they are not worth comparing. Even the worst-case scenario that the most cynical among us can imagine regarding having a lot of money would still be better than the experience of starvation caused by having no money.

The renowned songwriter and singer Bob Marley wrote: "In the abundance of water the fool is thirsty." Why does extreme poverty and starvation persist on a planet of abundance and in a world where some are worth so much—up to 129 billion dollars—that one person could be extremely wealthy? No single or simple answer applies to every situation. In some cases, people are prevented from reaching their potential through mental and physical oppression. This could be caused by oppressive government regimes within their countries or by international economic and political exploitation.

So if we remove the causes linked to external factors, what explanation remains if people continue to starve *in large* numbers? We must consider this from a deeply spiritual perspective. As human beings, we have a *responsibility* and a *necessity* to develop *skills* to harness the Earth's resources so that, at the very least, we can survive. This is a fundamental task that our human potential is fully capable of achieving, as shown by billions of people worldwide. It is widely believed that we only utilise, at most, ten per cent of our brains. However, even within this ten per cent, there is no space for failure, leading to extreme poverty and starvation. In general, and barring extraordinary external influences, poverty and hunger can be seen as conditions of *thought* and *feeling* that inhibit people's natural potential to meet their basic needs.

We are the only creatures on this planet that are at odds with nature. What does this mean? All other living beings have an innate instinct that aligns with nature's system of food and shelter. We must determine what to eat, how to provide suitable shelter, and design clothing to protect us from the elements. From our drive to achieve all of this, money became a reality. Money, as a tool, gained even greater importance because of our unique human ability. The capacity for diverse lifestyles has increased the importance we place on money. With the emergence of these varied lifestyles, we now have a greater need for services such as electricity, water, appliances, communication, entertainment, exercise equipment, swimming pools, and various types of machinery.

Nature says: ***Come, I have the sunshine, the rain, the seeds, the soil, the miracle of the seasons, and the wants and needs of people; come and do what you want with them. If you ignore or fail to utilise the season of opportunities, which is spring, then come autumn, you will reap what you have sown. If you haven't sown much, you will not reap much. If you sow nothing, you will reap nothing. In this scenario, our season of autumn becomes a season of winter, and we may feel compelled to plead with nature***

to produce what we had not planted or, worse, to change our crops from thorns to vibrant roses. Spring is truly an extraordinary season that brings an indescribable feeling of freshness, renewal, and change. We as humans must learn to take advantage when it arrives. Have a read of this beautiful description of spring that was paraphrased from columnist Chris Burns.

Nothing seems strong enough to erase the hope that spring brings. If for no other purpose, spring offers time for reflection - reflection on self, life, friendships, partnerships, family, relationships, money, nature, and sounds. Yes, spring provides an opportunity to combine these things to produce a mighty stew that can be as tasty and as satisfying to the human appetite for growth, advancement, acceptance, and fulfilment as any plate of fine food.

Poverty stems from failing to align with the abundance aspect of nature, which is the season of spring. Prosperity, on the other hand, results from connecting with the part of nature that says: bring me your labour, your imagination, your strong feelings, your values, and you will reap many rewards. As Jim Rohn said, ***"For every disciplined effort we get multiple rewards."*** This is commonly known as the law of sowing and reaping, or cause and effect. An often overlooked part of this law states: *not only will we reap what we have sown, but we will reap much more than what we have sown. If we plant a cup of wheat in spring, we will harvest a bushel of wheat in autumn.*

The law of cause and effect is impartial. It acts swiftly to produce both positive and negative results. Therefore, if people neglect to use their imagination, develop skills, and work together over a long-term, well-planned, disciplined effort to secure food supply, the consequence could be famine leading to severe starvation.

However, regardless of our actions, those who seek to educate *should not* promote any negative philosophies about the tool (money) that signifies our productivity, and those aiming to learn *should avoid* accepting such harmful teachings.

The relationship between reading, vocabulary, knowledge, behaviour, and success

Reading is the undisputed number one human activity that transforms our lives for the better.

"There is definitely a relationship between vocabulary and behaviour. The more limited the vocabulary, the more there is a tendency to poor behaviour." So says Jim Rohn in his audio presentation called "Take Charge of Your Life". This information came from a survey of prisoners in New England. Does it make sense that vocabulary would be related to behaviour? It does. Jim Rohn further stated, *"If you think about it for a while, it makes sense. Vocabulary is a way of seeing; one reason for vocabulary is to interpret what we see and hear. The vocabulary of the mind grapples with the words and the images that come to our minds. If you have a poor set of words, skills, and tools with which to interpret, you can imagine the errors and the mistakes you will make in judgment. And since vocabulary is a way of seeing, if you can't*

77

see well, you can imagine the errors you can make and how they will compound as life unfolds. "

MANY SELF-MADE INDIVIDUALS have achieved considerable financial success despite not being avid readers. However, these individuals likely utilised the power of having a strong, clear purpose or goal and possessed the discipline to persist and see it through. Having a well-defined purpose can similarly influence the mind to reading – it helps the mind find solutions to achieve its goals.

I have brought myself by long meditation to the conviction that a human being with a settled purpose must accomplish it, and that nothing can resist a will which will stake even existence upon its fulfilment. - Benjamin Disraeli

---

Having a clear purpose opens our minds, which in turn nurtures the emotions needed to pursue and embrace wealth. There is no place in this approach for negativity towards wealth. If negative feelings about money enter, our strong emotions may weaken, and our drive to succeed and achieve great things will decrease over time. Financial independence is a vital and noble goal. The lack of this goal becomes especially apparent and exaggerated in old age. Seeing an elderly person without dignity is genuinely heartbreaking.

To act on life's opportunities, we must accurately interpret what we see and hear, using our words and ideas. Since the rewards of opportunities are usually future outcomes, we also need a strong desire for the promised reward to keep us motivated and persistent until the goal is achieved. If the reward is riches, would we have the discipline and persistence if our perception of riches is negative? I don't think so. Most opportunities do not bring instant results; they require significant commitment, perseverance, and faith. This makes it crucial that we hold no negative beliefs that could weaken our efforts.

The fact that so few people who retire in wealthy countries are financially independent suggests that many have a poor relationship with money. But who's to say that negative beliefs about money—including widespread acceptance of dogma like "For the love of money is the root of all evil"—aren't partly to blame? To what extent do these negative beliefs, combined with a lack of financial and general knowledge, influence not only personal outcomes but also a country's overall prosperity?

John attended an event and started a conversation with an elderly man. During their chat, the man revealed he was experiencing financial difficulties and needed to sell his car. John agreed to examine the car in the parking lot.

So, what did he 'see'? He saw a car that looked outdated, being sold by an old man at a price he thought was high for an old vehicle. He declined, giving the false excuse that he didn't have the money.

Later, he saw a friend who appeared excited about something. His friend told him he had bought a car at a bargain price. He took him out to the parking lot and showed him the same car he had previously turned down.

He asked his friend why he would pay so much for such a car, and his friend explained that it was a Morgan. Now, the fact that he had refused the chance to buy that car showed he was unfamiliar with such vehicles, which is why he missed the opportunity. His friend revealed that the car was worth more than ten times what he had paid for it!

So, what do you think was John's reaction to his friend's realised opportunity? He suggested that his friend was lucky. But was this luck? No. He seized the chance because he possessed the knowledge to recognise what he saw.

John failed because he lacked the words to understand what he was looking at!

Are you now convinced about the power of words or vocabulary and the role they play in our lives? John suggested that his friend was lucky. So what exactly is luck? Take note of the following quote from the book, **"The Richest Man in Babylon", by George S. Clason:** *"The desire to be lucky is universal…we all hope to be favoured by the whimsical Goddess of Good Luck. Is there some way we can meet her and attract, not only her favourable attention but her generous favours? Is there a way to attract good luck?"*

The idea that luck is capricious is justified because so few can genuinely claim to be lucky. On a deeper level, the question arises about the origin of good luck. Is it some unfair advantage granted to only a few? If so, the next question is: who or what is responsible for bypassing the *natural cause-and-effect* processes of human actions? Some believe there is divine intervention. What are your thoughts?

A strong definition of luck is this: ***Luck occurs when preparedness meets opportunity.*** Opportunities are plentiful. Those of us who do not accept this are probably doing so because we have not been paying attention, or we have been listening to the wrong voices.

Listening to the wrong voices can lead to miseducation. Newspapers, for example, very rarely promote the virtue of property investment, yet property investment is the foundation of much wealth among the rich. Newspapers tend to sensationalise headlines about falling house prices and market crashes. Why do they do this? Negative headlines *sell newspapers,* and this is the business they are in!

Real education is the cornerstone of health, prosperity, and happiness

LUCK IS WHEN preparedness meets opportunity. So, how does one prepare to seize opportunities? We must prepare our minds to see life as it truly is. This involves avoiding the accumulation of false, negative beliefs about money and prosperity. We should prioritise gaining knowledge over simply accepting beliefs. Beliefs are easy to collect, but proper understanding takes effort. It's simple to absorb negative views about money, but reading the right books, listening to audio programs, and attending seminars that genuinely explain the true nature of money and wealth requires time and discipline—something many people avoid.

I've heard people dismiss authors who write about the principles of success by claiming they want to sell books or seminars to get rich, completely ignoring the value they might gain from the content. Some even argue that if the author is already wealthy, they should give away their books or run their seminars for free. This kind of thinking reveals a lack of understanding about the purpose and cost of real education. Too often, people overvalue formal education while undervaluing self-education. As Jim Rohn wisely said, *"Formal education will make you a living; self-education will make you a fortune."*

Real education is the realisation that we are in charge of life. If we don't take charge, life will take charge of us. It's common for people to ask, "How is life treating you?" I usually reply, "You mean, how am I treating life - who do you suppose is in charge?" Do you think someone with an attitude that they are in charge would stand a better chance of reaching their goals? Would you agree that if a person is financially independent, they have greater control over their life circumstances?

Proper education is recognising that although we can be self-sufficient, life functions best when we work together. Indeed, no man is an island. As Jim Rohn says, "It's hard to find a rich hermit."

Real education is the realisation that life or success seldom follows a straight path because, as the saying goes, "Life happens." There are often events and people competing for our attention and resources. Therefore, proper education involves understanding that sometimes we must focus and say "No" to those who demand our resources. It also includes learning how to cope with occasional tragedies and setbacks. Real education involves appreciating the role that money can play in providing us with peace of mind and the confidence to handle almost any of life's unforeseen expenses. In doing so, we plan to secure the necessary funds.

Real education involves accepting the adage, "As within, so without," which means that our outer life experiences reflect our *dominant* thoughts. Therefore, changing our way of thinking leads to changing our lives. With this in mind, we recognise how crucial it is to conduct thorough self-analysis and eliminate any negativity about money that we may have unintentionally accumulated.

Real education involves understanding that we shape the future through our thoughts and actions; the future is not predetermined. This realisation has helped those who were not born into wealth. **They unintentionally or deliberately embrace the philosophy in James Allen's book, "As a Man Thinketh," which wisely states, *"Man is the master of thought, the moulder of character, and the maker and shaper of condition, environment, and destiny."*** Within this statement lies the origin of profound wisdom. This wisdom does not see class or circumstances as barriers to achievement. However, it also serves as a warning by stating that we are the creators of our condition, environment, and destiny. Why is this a warning? Because if we accept this principle and take responsibility for shaping our financial situation, environment, and destiny, we must be mindful of our thoughts and feelings.

A close relative to the belief that circumstance and 'class' control our destiny is the idea that *inequality* is an inherent trait or, at best, a permanent condition. As a result, governments have debated and declared their intention to engineer it out of existence socially. Have they succeeded? Not in any significant way that we can observe. Why has there been such limited success? The answer lies in the size of the task and how well they understand the problem, as well as sometimes in the insincerity of intent.

Financial education needs to become a part of our national curriculum and scoring systems so that it's not just the rich kids that learn about money... it's all of us. – David Bach

---

The social engineering involved in making necessary societal changes includes reforming the education system to include financial education for the masses; it would also entail altering how people perceive money and wealth, which might involve revising biblical scriptures to reflect the truth. All of this would be a colossal task because governments consist of people, and as human beings, we are notorious for finding it challenging to change our thought patterns. Genuine education is when we are enlightened with the understanding that inequality exists only because we all differ in terms of *the quality of our thinking and the emotions that our thinking produces. And remember, most of our decisions are driven by emotion, and our choices and actions are what generate our results.*

Real education is the realisation that we will all spend the rest of our lives, and the thoughts and emotions we choose to embrace are consistently guiding us there. The question is whether our thoughts are leading us to a financial destiny that we will be happy with, or one filled with regrets.

We must dare to invent the future - Thomas Sankara

Real education involves recognising that there are five key aspects of life worth studying and striving to master: health, relationships, happiness, spirituality, and prosperity. It also means accepting that we are responsible for these five areas. A simple look at health, relationships, happiness, and spirituality shows how money can help us pursue these experiences. If you're still not convinced or cannot see the link between money and these aspects of life, remember that having enough cash allows us to manage our most valuable commodity better: time. Better control over our time is the foundation of freedom. With freedom, we can dedicate as much time as we want to these vital areas of life, which are available to all of us. Many of us might list things we'd like to do or places we'd like to visit, but our plans are often limited by time, often due to financial constraints.

Happiness, relationships, and health are skills that we need to develop, and it takes time to do so. Although we all have 24 hours, if the lack of financial independence means we must work for a significant part of that time, our happiness, relationships, and health can suffer. Our understanding of our spiritual nature, or the unseen part of our being, would also benefit from having enough *quality time* to think and research.

Proper education is understanding that our health is our most incredible wealth; therefore, it involves knowing what to ingest, what not to ingest, and what not to combine in the same meal to maintain good health. Good health is the foundation from which all valuable things arise. A friend of mine once told me that if he could afford it, he would buy more healthy foods. How many of us would opt for strictly organic foods if money were no object?

Have you ever wondered why some millionaires are not known for their academic achievements? Formal education has certain features that do not nurture the spirit and attitude typical of entrepreneurs. In a school system, failure can mean the end of the road. As a result, this system can create an extraordinary fear of failure. Successful people cannot have a strong aversion to taking risks.

In school, we learn that mistakes are bad, and we are punished for making them. Yet, if you look at the way humans are designed to learn, we learn by making mistakes. We learn to walk by falling down. If we never fell down, we would never walk. — Robert T. Kiyosaki, "Rich Dad, Poor Dad"

Real education involves recognising that failure is not always a permanent setback but often a temporary one. When Thomas Edison was conducting his experiments to invent the light bulb, he reached 5,000 attempts before someone suggested he should give up after failing so many times. He replied, "I have not failed 5,000 times. I have successfully identified 5,000 ways that don't work!" Do you believe money played a crucial role in his eventual success? Would it have been more challenging without the convenience of cash, like in a barter system?

Real education is wisdom, and wisdom teaches us that life is often a process of testing and elimination to discover what works and what doesn't. We learn this through studying and observing the lives of others, as well as from our own experiences. The purpose of this process is to find empirical evidence to support our conclusions.

Empirical (observational) evidence is more reliable than anecdotal (unverified) evidence. Anecdotal evidence can be misleading because it may be an aberration or exaggeration and, therefore, unlikely to produce the same result consistently. For example, there is strong empirical evidence that positive people generally achieve greater success than negative people. If, on occasion, a few negative individuals find success, does that prove negativity is effective?

Of course not. That's like citing a man who smoked until 90 but never developed cancer as proof that smoking doesn't cause cancer. Empirical evidence overwhelmingly suggests otherwise.

If, after doing some research, you find plenty of real-world examples that support the philosophy presented in this book, imagine how empowered you would feel. Adopting this kind of evidence-based knowledge and attitude toward money could be a transformative step toward a more successful and fulfilling life.

THE SIMPLEST MESSAGE I want to share through everything I have written so far is that we have been miseducated both intellectually and emotionally about money. On a deeper level, I want you to understand that our thoughts and emotions are the most powerful tools we possess, capable of either destroying us or freeing us. On an even deeper spiritual level, our *thoughts* are part of the fabric of the universe; they shape the direction and destination of our lives. This is what Earl Nightingale calls 'the strangest secret'. It's a 'secret' because no instruction manual came with us at birth. All the dynamics of life are something we have to figure out. Now, read an excerpt from Earl Nightingale's record called "The Strangest Secret".

The strangest secret

For twenty years, I looked for the key which would determine what would happen to a human being. Was there a key, I wanted to know, which would make the future a promise that we could foretell to a large extent? Was there a key that could guarantee a person becoming successful if he only knew about it and knew how to use it? Well, there is such a key and I've found it. Here is the key to success and the key to failure: we become what we think about! Throughout all of history, the great wise men and teachers, philosophers and prophets have disagreed with one another on many different things. It is only on this one point that they are in complete and unanimous agreement.

Buddha said, 'All we are is what we have thought about.' Marcus Aurelius said, 'A man's life is what his thoughts make of it.' Ralph Waldo Emerson said this, 'A man is what he thinks about all day long.' William James said, 'The greatest discovery of my generation is that human beings can alter their lives by altering their attitude of mind.' And George Bernard Shaw said, 'People are always blaming their circumstances for what they are. I don't believe in circumstances. The people who get on in this world are the people who get up and look for the circumstances they want, and if they can't find them, they make them.' It stands to reason that the person who is thinking about a definite and worthwhile goal is going to reach it, because that's what he is thinking about, and we become what we think about. Conversely, the man who has no goal, who doesn't know where he is going, and whose thoughts must therefore be thoughts of confusion, anxiety, fear and worry, becomes what he thinks about — his life becomes one of frustration, fear, anxiety and worry. And if he thinks about nothing, he becomes nothing.

The human mind is the last great unexplored continent on earth. It contains riches beyond our wildest dreams. It will return anything we plant in it...the very law that gives us success is a two-edged sword; we must control our thinking! The same rule that can lead a man to a life of success, wealth, happiness and all the things he has dreamed of for himself and his family, that very same law can lead him into the gutter. It's all in how he uses it, for good or for bad. This is the strangest secret in the world.

Did you find any truth in the philosophies above? If so, the question you should ask yourself is this: What if I plant deep-seated emotions in my mind, such as the belief that the love of money is the root of all evil, or that rich people are crooks, ruthless, immoral, and unhappy? What if I combine this with a belief that financial success will bring problems, like losing friends and increasing life's difficulties? What should I expect my mind to produce after cultivating such a mixture of negative beliefs about something vital to me? Would it lead to prosperity and freedom, or to scarcity, endless struggles, or merely getting by?

The abundant universe is for everyone.

Given the power of institutions that spread lies and miseducation about money, we need words and ideas to challenge these deeply rooted false beliefs. We must recalibrate our minds and emotions to adopt an attitude towards money that aligns with the *truth* of what money truly is. Truth is sweeter than wine! Truth is the sweetest nectar – it forms the fabric of everything that makes our lives function well. Lies and miseducation are substances that create delusion and illusion, and they are never based on correct principles. Correct principles are those that align with the universe, which exudes abundance. Scarcity is a man-made concept.

Some people question this because they've seen drought and assume nature is lacking. But in truth, nature is abundant—there has never been a shortage of water on the planet as a whole. The same goes for money: it isn't scarce globally, only unevenly distributed. Likewise, while certain places receive less sunlight, you've never seen a sunset hold back. The sun shines fully on everything within its reach. So, droughts and dim skies exist, but only in isolated parts of the Earth, not like Earth itself. Interestingly, we don't talk about a 'sunshine drought' in areas with limited sunlight. And this provides a clue to achieving prosperity: move within a range where ideas can brighten your mind with positivity about wealth. This involves reading, listening to personal development talks or recordings, and seeking out people who maintain a healthy, positive attitude towards money and prosperity.

About his salary, the man said, "This is all they pay!" And the philosopher responded, "No, this is all they pay YOU! Don't they pay some people in your company a lot more?" –Jim Rohn.

Suppose you are a young person just beginning your financial journey. In that case, if you are a late starter or if you are starting over after an economic disaster, I must caution you: Be careful, because the philosophy and attitude you adopt regarding money will make all the difference in your financial journey and destination. Be cautious, as life is not a practice run, and as far as we know, it is not a rehearsal for something else; therefore, the philosophy and attitude you adopt towards money will be like the set of the sail on your financial ship, guiding you unerringly to your destination. Remember, your financial journey and destination will significantly influence your overall quality of life, so cultivate and maintain a positive attitude towards money.

Therefore, as you begin your new or renewed financial journey, I recommend that you incorporate the following truths into your philosophy and attitude—truths that have been central to this book: the statement "For the love of money is the root of all evil" is not accurate. It doesn't matter whether it's written in the Bible or comes from another source. We communicate through language, and language must follow some rules of meaning, or else we would not be able to function effectively with each other. Ideas must be guided by practical application, logic, intelligence, and wisdom.

This dogma that the love of money is evil does not align with those standards. In truth, most of the worst evil acts committed in the world have nothing to do with loving money. Beyond the many heinous acts of paedophilia, rape, and murder—none of which are motivated by money—some nations sponsor terrorism of the gravest kind purely for ideological reasons or a thirst for power. And the desire for power is not necessarily the same as the desire for money.

The entire fabric of our existence is governed by Natural Science, which is characterised by laws, principles, and logic. Natural Science includes all sciences that are not man-made, such as gravity or the workings of our bodies. Therefore, whatever or whoever we consider responsible for our existence must also possess qualities of logic, laws, and principles. How can something or someone perform consistently in a logical manner yet not be logical by nature? With this reasoning, you should be able to dismiss "For the love of money is the root of all evil" as not originating from such a source.

You must take responsibility for understanding this truth because religion may not change its dogma about money anytime soon. That said, regardless of whether they alter their views, you cannot rely on religious organisations—or Hollywood—for securing your financial future, since that is not their purpose.

Hollywood primarily aims to entertain; it is not an institution for education or enlightenment. Religious dogma tends to focus on doctrines about the 'afterlife', offering little emphasis on the practicality of living and enjoying this present life. There is also minimal focus on contributing to the improvement of our earthly experience. This is why some religious organisations even instruct their members not to vote.

If you are one of those who are determined to hold on to this dogma because you accept it as God's words, I would suggest that you at least take into consideration that the Bible has been rewritten many times. The apparent truth of this is demonstrated by the fact that we now use the King James *Version*, and there are other translations or *versions* of this Bible being used today. So, you could choose the option to assume at least that 'the love of money' dogma is a mistranslation, and perhaps you should campaign to have it modified in the interest of truth. I hope this book will serve as part of this campaign. I think it would benefit the Christian world enormously if this scripture were corrected to read, "For the love of money is the root of **some** evil." Christianity would also benefit from promoting the positive scriptures within the Bible about money.

We now face a situation where numerous scriptural discrepancies exist between the *New American Standard Bible,* the *New World Translation Bible,* and the *King James Version* (KJV) of the Bible. For instance, the KJV states in John 10:30, "I and **my** Father are one," while the *New American Standard Bible* reads, "I and **the** Father are one." This indicates disagreements over the correct translation of the original texts. In some cases, entire verses are omitted in the newer translations mentioned above. For example, part of Luke 4:8, "Get thee behind me, Satan," appears in the KJV but is absent from the *New American Standard Bible.* All of this underscores that revising the phrase "the love of money" to reflect truth and accuracy better is far from being a ridiculous suggestion.

Money and prosperity are *neutral*; they don't care who embraces them, so do not taint a person's achievement, even if they have poor morals. Taint the *person*! From this, I want to re-emphasise the importance of dropping the blame game and taking responsibility for our morals and actions. Our happiness is within our control because it depends on our thoughts and the emotions we cultivate. Our joy can be significantly boosted when we take advantage of the many lifestyle options available to us, and money is the lubricant that makes this possible.

Hollywood's portrayal of the wealthy does not reflect the true meaning of being rich. Relying on such a distorted example to form opinions and attitudes towards wealthy people is misleading. Be aware that Hollywood will continue to dramatise and exaggerate what it means to be affluent, and whatever truth they present will depict only a small minority. Therefore, do not internalise their negative portrayals of wealth as a universal truth. Remember, financial independence is a beautiful and desirable goal – it shows that you are a valuable contributor to your country's economy and that you have added value to others; it indicates disciplined habits and ambition, which are all admirable qualities.

Learn how to spend money on treasures.

It has been understood that a significant purpose of money is to improve the quality of our life's journey. Achieving this requires us to practice the art of living well. Living well is a skill we develop to shape and choose our lifestyle. A worthwhile lifestyle involves learning how to spend our money wisely. This may sound unusual because everyone knows how to 'spend' money. Now, I will suggest spending money on things I consider to be treasures that can enrich your life's journey. The first and most obvious treasure to invest in is quality books that inspire, instruct, and help you grow mentally and emotionally. These silent partners are treasures that can also educate, inspire, and support your children's mental and emotional growth. This legacy could potentially benefit future generations as well. You can initiate this by showing your children you value reading and encouraging them to see the benefits of reading.

When I was 12 years old, I took a coloured school photo for an identification card. Some years later, I lost this photo. Now, as an adult, I realise that it was the only coloured photograph I had from that time, and I remember it with great regret. Since then, I have often heard my late mentor, the great Jim Rohn, speak about the value of having many photos to tell our life story, and that these should be treasures we leave behind. I deeply connect with this sentiment and reflect on my regret at not having photos of some of my family members, such as my great-grandparents and grandparents.

Such photos would be an incredible treasure for me, as well as for current and future generations. Wouldn't it be wonderful if you had hundreds of photos documenting your family history? I am poorer for it because many records of my family are missing. I do not even have a photo of any of my father's family. Aside from the fact that I never met any of them—except for a cousin—I have no photos of either his mother or father.

This is about using modern technology to record the sequences of our lives. There is no reason for any of us not to own a digital camera, especially compared to the 1970s, when only a few could afford cameras. We now have an extra device to help us preserve memories — a camcorder. So, invest in these tools to gather treasures in your life. Would it be an incredible treasure to have moving images that document key moments from childhood to the present?

Should you neglect to record your children's lives so they can enjoy this treasure as adults?

Do you know what I fantasise about? I imagine the joy it would bring if I had video recordings of myself at school, in my classrooms, and various other scenes from my childhood to adolescence. It would be even more extraordinary and mind-blowing if similar recordings were made of my siblings, my parents, and others. What an incredible treasure this would be! We can turn this into a reality for our children and future generations by investing time and resources in these tools.

Another excellent reason to use our cameras and camcorders is to capture images of the places we have lived and visited, both at home and abroad. Have you ever seen pictures of places you know that were taken, say, 50 years ago? Did you find the changes and transformation interesting? So, record videos and take photographs of your home and neighbourhood. These will be interesting to your children and relatives. Any life worth living is also worth documenting. So, take pictures of everything, including the cars you have driven. Hopefully, you are not one of those people who are more interested in taking photos of your pet than of your own life.

LIFESTYLE IS THE key difference between providing your children with the best education and struggling to afford only the cheapest options. It distinguishes living in a hovel, a house, or a mansion; having one bathroom or multiple to suit your needs; travelling economy, business, or first class; eating cheap, unhealthy food or nourishing health foods; finding time for relaxation or constantly working one or two jobs; seeing your family frequently or rarely; and being able to help those in need or needing assistance yourself. These choices are available, and money empowers us to select options aligned with our aspirations. For most of us, we live in a way our income allows; we do not always live according to our dreams and aspirations.

Whatever is holding us back, we need to identify it and eliminate it. We must wage a relentless war on any negativity that does not serve us. For those of you who have conflicts with the pursuit of 'material' things and are on a deep quest to understand the purpose of life, it may be helpful to consider Earl Nightingale's statement about human purpose. He wisely said, "We are here to serve each other." I also believe that given the intricate design and beauty of our bodies, minds, the earth, and the universe, we can reasonably assume that we should enjoy this human experience. Additionally, considering the capacity of our brains and minds, we are intended to expand their use, thereby broadening and enriching our enjoyment and experiences. Do you think that if you grow and extend your abilities, you could bring more value to the marketplace than you do now and, in so doing, provide goods or services to many more people?

Building on this deep thought, I recognise that we are mental and spiritual beings having a human experience. This human journey is beautiful and deserves to be enhanced and expanded to the best of our abilities. Money is a *neutral, convenient, and necessary* tool that we use to improve this experience. *It is essential because, mainly, it covers the basics of food, clothing, and shelter.* Therefore, we have a choice; we can either conform to dogmas, ideas, and stories about money that aren't based on truth, or we can embrace the truth and let it liberate us. What have you decided? Remember, it's unwise to spend most of your life working for something you do not love, especially since it is so intertwined with every aspect of your life. The choice is yours, and the time to decide is now. Do you want to only get by, or are you going to go for all you can achieve?

Remember, it is not just what you achieve that holds the greatest value; it is *the person you become in the process of pursuing everything you desire that has this value.* Enduring happiness is rooted in the inner self that we develop and evolve through pushing ourselves beyond limits. One way we drive ourselves is by adding value to the lives of others, which can include providing goods and services to the marketplace. Do you believe this is a noble and vital philosophy for the continuation and progress of civilisation? Should we all contribute to the human effort, or do you prefer to go unnoticed?

How would you like to be remembered by your family, friends, or community? What about leaving a lasting legacy as someone who contributed greatly by funding the best education for your children and supporting the education of others? Or being remembered as someone who left your community in a much better state than you found it? If these ideas seem too ambitious, you could be remembered as a person who did their best by exploring and testing all their abilities. Surely, you understand that your abilities are an essential part of your spiritual self. Have you thought about who you truly are? Have you concluded that you are a spiritual being having a human experience, and therefore, everything you do is spiritual?

Have you realised that earning money comes from utilising the mental, spiritual, and invisible energy that defines you? We can transform this energy into knowledge, creativity, and effort, which we use to obtain food, clothing, shelter, and a livelihood. As you already know, this is what money ultimately signifies. So, once again, are you going to diminish our most noble energy, love, by linking it to the basest thoughts and actions we call evil?

Once you have connected your spiritual abilities with earning money, should you indulge in your capacity to provide goods and services to others? I am inclined to indulge. What about you?

End